T0318945

Cambridge Elements ≡

Elements in Histories of Emotions and the Senses
edited by
Jan Plamper
Goldsmiths, University of London

EMOTION, SENSE, EXPERIENCE

Rob Boddice
Freie Universität Berlin

Mark Smith
University of South Carolina

CAMBRIDGE
UNIVERSITY PRESS

CAMBRIDGE
UNIVERSITY PRESS

University Printing House, Cambridge CB2 8BS, United Kingdom

One Liberty Plaza, 20th Floor, New York, NY 10006, USA

477 Williamstown Road, Port Melbourne, VIC 3207, Australia

314–321, 3rd Floor, Plot 3, Splendor Forum, Jasola District Centre, New Delhi – 110025, India

79 Anson Road, #06–04/06, Singapore 079906

Cambridge University Press is part of the University of Cambridge.

It furthers the University's mission by disseminating knowledge in the pursuit of education, learning, and research at the highest international levels of excellence.

www.cambridge.org
Information on this title: www.cambridge.org/9781108813631
DOI: 10.1017/9781108884952

First published 2020

A catalogue record for this publication is available from the British Library.

ISBN 978-1-108-81363-1 Paperback
ISSN 2632–1068 (online)
ISSN 2632-105X (print)

Emotion, Sense, Experience

Elements in Histories of Emotions and the Senses

DOI: 10.1017/9781108884952
First published online: October 2020

Rob Boddice
Freie Universität Berlin

Mark Smith
University of South Carolina

Author for correspondence: Rob Boddice, rob.boddice@gmail.com

Abstract: *Emotion, Sense, Experience* calls on historians of emotions and the senses to come together in serious and sustained dialogue. The Element outlines the deep if largely unacknowledged genealogy of historical writing insisting on a braided history of emotions and the senses; explains why recent historical treatments have sometimes profitably but nonetheless unhelpfully segregated the emotions from the senses; and makes a compelling case for the heuristic and interpretive dividends of bringing emotions and sensory history into conversation. Ultimately, we envisage a new way of understanding historical lived experience generally, as a mutable product of a situated world–brain–body dynamic. Such a project necessarily points us towards new interdisciplinary engagement and collaboration, especially with social neuroscience. Unpicking some commonly held assumptions about affective and sensory experience, we reimagine the human being as both biocultural and historical, reclaiming the analysis of human experience from biology and psychology and seeking new collaborative efforts.

Keywords: history of experience, history of emotions, history of the senses, interdisciplinarity, social neuroscience

ISBNs:9781108813631 (PB), 9781108884952 (OC)
ISSNs: 2632-1068 (online), 2632-105X (print)

Contents

1 Entanglement, Divergence

When we first met, at the research seminar hosted by Constance Classen and David Howes at Concordia University in Montreal in 2017, we immediately tapped into a sense of shared critical frustration about our respective fields, the history of emotions and the history of the senses. This has developed into what we hope will be received as a pointed intervention, to some a provocation, that aims to reorientate scholarship in these fields towards a new history of experience, or at least to explore its possibilities. But insofar as we aim to innovate, we feel it is also important to share our converging criticisms, as well as pointing out where we feel there is a substantial platform upon which to build. On the one hand, we could not fathom how, given the historical contingency of both 'emotional' and 'sensory' experience and knowledge, these two fields could be so separate. Certainly, they were not always so, but it seems a fair assessment that much of the recent literature in the history of emotions has been unaware of the parallel work going on in the history of the senses, and, we think, *vice versa*. So, we wanted to join forces, but to what end? It seemed to us that historians of the emotions and historians of the senses were both trying to get at isolated facets of the same thing – experience – but could only see part of the picture. To be more critical, in focusing on ring-fenced categories – 'emotions' and 'senses' – they were risking anachronism, or a kind of archival blindness to the ways in which historical experience was constructed out of situated feelings, admixtures of situated historical affective categories that do not make sense considered simply as 'emotion' or 'sense'. These discrete categories are reflections of both academic and popular psychology's recent past, which has formalised both 'basic emotions' and the canonical 'five senses'. While we are not calling for the end of either sensory or emotions histories – for there is still much more to be learned from discrete scholarship in both fields – we are nevertheless calling for their dialogue. Should this not occur, we believe the central interpretive contributions of each field will not only begin to etiolate but that we will end up denying ourselves access to a more accurate, robust and, ultimately, more meaningful history of human experience. As will become clear, there has been, in recent years, significant disruption of these categories within psychological research, but the more simplistic view remains popular and it has, perhaps unwittingly, overly determined the research goals of historians who are interested in emotions and senses in the past.

What was remarkable to us was that this very criticism existed right at the beginning of a formal attempt to fashion both the history of emotions and the history of the senses. It has not been well observed. Lucien Febvre, about whom more to follow, reflected in 1938 that contemporary Western psychological categories could not possibly work for other times and places, since *mentalités* were wrapped up with local and temporal contingencies. General schemes would always be more revealing of the present than the past, front-loaded with anachronism.

Searching for the origins of work braiding emotion and the senses is not an especially profitable enterprise: antecedents always exist. Still, it is worth dwelling on some of the earliest professional historical work on emotion, the senses and experience which called for precisely the sort of examination we undertake here – not least because, first, there was genuine and usable insight in this work, insight which we think enduring and valuable; and, second, because, as Bettina Hitzer (2020a) has recently, and correctly, remarked, it is 'dumbfounding' that more has not been made of these insights generally, especially in light of recent work on the biocultural history of the body.

If we sensibly hesitate to identify a 'first' we nevertheless happily locate early gestures calling for the inclusion of the sensate and emotion. One such gesture is found in the work of the influential Dutch historian, Johan Huizinga (1872–1945).[1] Critically, Huizinga was preoccupied with trying to better understand the idea of human experience, a principal aim of our work here. A founder of modern cultural history, Huizinga (2009) brought to bear a concern with recognising the importance of what David Howes terms 'historical sensation', particularly during the Middle Ages and Renaissance (Howes, 2018a, vol. 2, 2; Otterspeer, 2010). Frank Ankersmit (2018) has paid particular attention to the sensory and emotive language and content of Huizinga's work and maintains that Huizinga's attention to the senses and emotion, particularly in his influential 1919 work, *Herfsttij der Middeleeuwen: Studie Over Levens-en Gedachtenvormen der Veertiende en Vijftiende Eeuw in Frankkrijk en de Nederlanden* (*The Autumn of the Middle Ages*; alternatively titled, *The Waning of the Middle Ages*) was a product of his training as a linguist and his keen interest in the Dutch literary genre of sensitivism. Huizinga believed that to capture historical experience the historian had to think in terms of historical sensation. The temporal and local situation of that sensation, however (and, given the nature of his later work, perhaps oddly), was not important to Huizinga here; he was simply concerned to establish the idea of how emotion and the senses might work together to inform and articulate human experience. Huizinga's understanding of historical experience was predicated on that moment when, notes Ankersmit, 'spatial and temporal demarcations have momentarily been lifted; it is as if the temporal trajectory between past and present, instead of separating the two, has become the locus of

---

[1] There are any number of historians we could identify here. We elect to light on just three whose work best exemplifies the points we take to be foundational to our project. For other work of importance, see Smith, forthcoming; Boddice, 2018a, 8–32.

their encounter. Historical experience pulls the faces of past and present together in a short but ecstatic kiss' (vol. 2, 24). Sounds especially grant us access to what Huizinga considered a deeper understanding of human experience. Trying to fathom the sounds of the past and how people heard them – the meaning people attached to what they heard – was an exercise in historical intimacy and Huizinga believed that a thoroughly decontextualised approach and appeal to language was key to accessing this understanding. Huizinga relied heavily on synesthetic metaphor in an effort to grasp what we might think of as the feel of an age. In the late French and Dutch Middle Ages, 'Life was so bright and colorful, it bore the scent of blood and roses' [*Zoo fel en bont was het leven, zoo verdroeg het den geur van bloed en rozen dooreen*] (Huizinga, 1919, 18). Here, Huizinga relies on the interplay between sight and smell in an effort to capture the sensory atmospherics of a place, people and time. Huizinga used language as a medium to convey the sensate past but not without cost. As Ankersmit says: 'historical experience and contextualization mutually exclude each other' (vol. 2, 27) in *The Autumn of the Middle Ages*; the Dutch historian stripped away the distracting gauze of historiography and relied very heavily on language alone to bridge the 'sound or the smell of the past' and interpret its emotional meaning for not just people in the past but also for writers in the present (vol. 2, 29). Huizinga's experiment was short-lived: a decade later he abandoned his heavy reliance on language alone.[2] In essence, Huizinga gave us a good basis and justification for needing to think about how central the senses and emotions were to understanding human experience in the past but he left us wanting when it came to how best to access that understanding.

A number of scholars have highlighted the importance of Lucien Febvre, the eminent French historian and member of the influential *Annales* school of historical inquiry, for the foundation of the history of emotions and the history of the senses (Hitzer, 2020a; Boddice, 2018a; Plamper, 2015; Smith, forthcoming; Rosenfeld, 2011; Dixon, 2011), but few have observed his call for a greater dialogue between emotions and senses. In 1941, Febvre spoke explicitly about the '*vie affective*'. Central to Febvre's understanding of this life – one constituted by the braiding of the senses and emotions – is the highly context-specific idea and language of *sensibilité*. Febvre insists, for example, that in the seventeenth century (in France, at least), *sensibilité* was deployed when attempting to identify impressions of a moral quality, viz. a *sensibilité* towards the truth. In the following century, says Febvre, 'the word refers to a particular way of experiencing human feelings – feelings of pity, sadness, etc'. The word '*sensible*'

---

[2] On Huizinga's shift from experience to sensation, see Howes, 2018a, 2; Huizinga, 1984. The basis of Huizinga's essay was first given as a speech in 1926 and then published in 1929.

captured this set of feelings and was, he says, increasingly distinguished from the quality of '*tendre*' [passionate, affectionate]. Added to this was a more recent understanding that treats *sensibilité* as a property of the nervous system which receives impressions – such as sensory perception and experience. For Febvre (1973, 13), *sensibilité* was a context-specific word used to understand 'the emotional life of man and all its manifestations' ('la vie affective et ses manifestations').

To be sure, in this essay at least, Febvre (1973) spends rather more time deliberating on how historians can attend to emotion as an historical subject than he does on the senses. But what he says about the history of emotion here is worth exploring in some detail. 'In the first instance', writes Febvre, 'an *emotion* is certainly not the same thing as a mere *automatic* reaction of the organism to an external stimuli [sic]' (13). Instead, emotions have 'a particular character which no man concerned with the social life of other men can any longer disregard' (14). In an important respect, emotional life is part and parcel of an intellectual life, a form of expression of consciousness. 'Intellectual activity presupposes social life', he argues, and it is in the realm of the emotional life that 'the initial ground for . . . inter-individual relations between the consciousness of men' is located (15). His understanding of history is at times unhelpfully framed in zero-sum fashion which posits the emergence of intellectual life at the expense of emotion but even here he is careful to qualify and stresses that context might well allow for interplay between the emotions and intellect.

Take, for example, his critique of Huizinga. The Dutch historian, argued Febvre, was clumsy, using entirely too broad a brush to characterize entire epochs – such as the Middle Ages – as almost exclusively wedded to a limited number of forms of emotional expression: anger, violence, impulsivity. To Huizinga's poetic claim that the late Middle Ages was 'too violent and so contrasting that it had the mixed smell of blood and roses', Febvre replies: 'Well, all this is quite well and even attractively put, but, nevertheless, it leaves a certain disquiet in the reader. Is it in fact sound work?' (16–17). Febvre says it is not simply because he believes that no era or even society can be reduced to one or even a limited set of emotional signatures. The effective (and affective) historian, says Febvre, details the interaction among the emotions and hesitates to consign vast swaths of the past to a particular sensory or emotional category. Simply put, says Febvre, Huizinga poses his historical problem 'out of context' (18). Understanding the meaning of emotion (and, by extension, the senses) in the context in which they circulated is critical, maintains Febvre. Febvre calls for historians to borrow what they can from cognate disciplines to achieve this reading, notably psychology:

If from the outset we can lean firmly on the latest critical and positive achievements of our neighbours the psychologists, then we might, I feel, be able to undertake a whole series of studies none of which have yet been done, and as long as they have not been done *there will be no real history possible.* No history of love, just remember that. We have no history of death. We have no history of pity, or of cruelty. We have no history of joy. (24; his emphasis)

As we suggest in the following, Febvre was on to something important in this call for cross-disciplinary fertilization and emotion.

Febvre also took the senses seriously. Indeed, to demonstrate his central thesis about the nature of religious belief in the sixteenth century, he was obliged to think carefully about the sensate. If Huizinga used language to gesture broadly to the sensory atmospherics of an era, Febvre examined the senses of necessity because he believed it was one of the main ways in which he could explain the context-specific nature of the mental world of the sixteenth century.

Febvre (1947, 424–33, 438; English translation, 1982, 423–32, 437) saw the senses and emotions as interlaced. In his 1947 work, *Le problème de l'incroyance au XVIe siècle. La religion de Rabelais,* Febvre maintained that 'men' of the sixteenth century (in his hands, they were always male), were people of 'feeling' [*sentant*] because of their sensory environment and their engagement with it. 'We are hothouse plants; those men grew out of doors', he argued: 'They were men close to the earth and to rural life, who encountered the countryside even in their cities, its plants and animals, its smells and noises' (1982, 427) [nous sommes des hommes de serre ; ils étaient des plein-vent. Des hommes proches de la terre et de la vie rurale. Des hommes qui, dans leurs cités même, retrouvaient la campagne, ses bêtes et ses plantes, ses odeurs et ses bruits (1947, 428)]. They were 'open-air men, seeing nature but also feeling, sniffing, hearing, touching, breathing her through all her senses' (427) [Des hommes de plein air, voyant mais sentant aussi, humant, écoutant, palpant, aspirant la nature par tous leurs sens (1947, 428)]. This is not the place to offer a formal critique of Febvre's reading: there is quite a lot wrong with it, in fact (it assumes a uniformity among all classes of sensory experience, for example). But whatever the shortcomings of Febvre's treatment of the senses, his brush was not so frustratingly broad as Huizinga's and Febvre was careful to contextualize his understanding. Place and time mattered. More than that, Febvre also thought in multisensory terms, treating sound, smell and touch as intimately related and unfriendly to disaggregation. He properly treated the past as a multisensory and even intersensory universe, something that sensory history has recently taken up in earnest (Howes, 2018a, vol. 2, 2; Smith, forthcoming; 2007). Imprecise though it was, Febvre's treatment of religion in the sixteenth century happily and compellingly incorporated appeals to emotion, the senses, and, critically, context.

Febvre's thinking reached fuller refinement in the work of Alain Corbin, arguably the modern founder of the history of the senses and also an astute observer of the history of emotion. Corbin wrote not simply of the sensate past – although that is often his focus – but on how emotion and the senses worked in tandem to reflect and actively help create the context of historical experience. This much is apparent from Corbin's (1995) *Time, Desire, and Horror: Toward a History of the Senses*, as well as from his other work, in which he theorizes the writing of the history of the senses and emotions.

The senses, he suggests, are inextricable to emotions: horror, desire, any number of emotions, were indexed to sensory experiences and hitched to a specific context. 'There is no other way', writes Corbin, 'to know men of the past than by trying to borrow their glasses and to live their emotions' [connaître les hommes du passé qu'en essayant d'emprunter leurs lunettes et de vivre leurs émotion] (Corbin, 2000, 67; Godfrey 2002, 387). Smells, sounds, touches, sensory experiences generally, informed the emotional cadence of a particular people at a given time and it is Corbin's firm belief that we cannot understand those experiences outside the context in which they were experienced. Corbin was convinced that to access the past, historians needed to embrace evidence from all sources and multiple genres. Literature, poetry especially, could be helpful not as a source of empirical proof but, rather, in its discursive power; a careful appreciation of the environment, read broadly, was also useful in helping situate emotion and the senses; and psychology, properly applied, granted historians access to shifting modes of perception. On the potential of psychology especially to inform the history of emotion, the senses and experience, Corbin was on to something, as we demonstrate in the following and as a few other historians have also suggested. Still, all had to be handled with care in an effort to avoid unwitting anachronism. Context reigns supreme for Corbin and any disciplinary borrowing had to bend to the historian's utter insistence on the preeminent importance of understanding time, place and constituency (Corbin, 1995, 183). It is these insights (although still an admittedly underdeveloped intellectual architecture) which inform our understanding of the history of experience and allow us to push for a more robust, articulated and rigorous way of thinking about emotion, the senses and human historical experience (Corbin, 1995, 183 esp.; Godfrey, 2002, 387; Parr, 2010, 189 esp.; Smith, 2010).

Since the 1980s, writing on the history of the senses and the history of emotion has diverged, the early braiding of the two fields apparent in the work of Corbin and others gradually evaporating. The result has been a quarantining with histories of emotion becoming increasing insensitive to the history of the senses and sensory history rarely even gesturing towards the emotional register of its work. Why this has been the case is not entirely clear and it is possible that there is more than one cause. Part of the explanation is field-contingent: emotion and sensory history have had their own interpretive imperatives. It may also be the case that the unfortunate divergence is also reflective of more systemic changes in the structure of the historical profession generally.

Historians of emotion, especially at the beginning of the second wave of emotions research beginning in the mid-1980s, appear to have discounted sustained and meaningful engagement with the senses in favour of speaking to a contemporary psychological debate about emotions concerning nature versus nurture, cognitive versus non-cognitive, and the universal as opposed to the situationally constructed. At that point, exacerbated by the ongoing existence of psychohistory, which most mainstream historians would eventually come to reject, these questions were essentially deferred. Nature (or biology), so the argument went, was not the historian's remit, and that meant focusing on culturally contingent *expressions* of emotion.[3] The corollary was the implicit adoption of a psychological orthodoxy of emotional categories, essentially surrendering the field of emotion knowledge production to psychologists, rendering history a subfield in the conversation and consigning historians to work within contemporary psychology's emotion categories (which is precisely what Febvre warned against). The net effect has been to steer historians of emotion away from due consideration of the senses.[4] Historians of emotions continue to raise the nature/nurture, constructivist/universalist debate, but rarely do they break out of orthodox psychological framing of what emotions *are*. And this blinds them not only to the historiography of the senses, but to the senses per se.

If psychology hobbled emotions history in this way, the heavy influence of sensory anthropology in the writing of sensory history should have ensured that

---

[3] See, for example Stearns and Stearns, 1986, 4–8. The Stearns never showed any love for psychohistory, but its importance was evident in the framing of their (1988) edited volume, *Emotion and Social Change: Toward a New Psychohistory.* Following the intellectual thread all the way down to Susan J. Matt and Peter N. Stearns (2013), one finds no mention of the senses at all. For a general account of the development of Peter Stearns' ideas in the history of emotions, see Olsen and Boddice, 2017.

[4] Most histories of emotion simply ignore the senses altogether. For a recent example where an engagement with the history of the senses seemed both necessary, even obvious, but was nonetheless essentially missing, see Downes, Holloway, and Randles, (2018). Jan Plamper (2015) puts Febvre squarely in the frame, but aside from a single footnote (295*n*170) offering a 'few examples which link the history of the senses with the history of emotion', the thread is dropped. The senses make no substantial appearance at all in Rosenwein and Cristiani, 2018.

histories of the senses continued to engage fully with the emotions. After all, the foundational work of sensory anthropologists was always closely and personally related to historical research. We are thinking of David Howes (1989; 1990; 1991; 2018a; 2018b) and Constance Classen, (1993a; 1993b; 1997; 1998; 2014; Classen and Howes, 2006) here especially. They continually suggested the importance not only of emotion to the historical study of the senses but also recognized the desirability of a (historically contextualized) incorporation of the natural sciences into studies of the sensate, very much along the lines we are calling for in this Element.[5]

Although emotion is sometimes still apparent in some sensory histories, it largely plays a distant second fiddle; moreover, some sensory histories have forgotten the valuable calls for a fully context-sensitive sensory scholarship championed by Febvre, Corbin, Howes and Classen especially.[6] Whether or not these missteps are a function of faulty memory, a lack of familiarization with earlier scholarship, or down to changes within the historical profession at large remains unclear. The historical profession's increasing calls for interdisciplinarity are often honoured by sensory historians and much to the benefit of all. That much said, given this tendency, it is odd to see that the key insights offered by sensory anthropology have been taken on board by sensory history only partially and sometimes not at all. Perhaps other pressures within the historical profession better explain why sensory history has tended to not only sidestep emotions history but also sometimes court a certain anachronism. Institutional calls for 'relevance' – for history to be made more accessible, popular, and, in effect, consumable – invite a heavily decontextualized historical sensory writing, where sensory literary flourish improperly stands in for sustained contextualized analysis. Some of the most popular books on, for example, the US Civil War are rife with animating sounds, smells and tastes, yet frequently fail to tell readers what was meant, historically, by those same sounds, smells and tastes (Smith, 2015, 4–5). Professional pressures have also led historians of all persuasions, sensory ones included, to write about ever-smaller slivers of historical space and time. If the deliberately ecumenical approach of the *Annales* sensory history school helped invite and stimulate considerations of emotions and psychology, the more narrow and professionally inspired focus of some subsequent writing on the history of the senses tells us about the costs of research in the modern university setting. Febvre and Corbin may well have been less hostage to the pressure of specialization and the dividend of their work

---

[5] See Howes, 2018b. In the 1990s, both Classen and Howes kept alive the emotion/senses/natural science dialogue. See Classen, 1993a; 1993b; 1997; 1998; Classen, Howes, and Synnott, 1994; Howes, 1989; 1991; 1990.

[6] Quick access to examples may be found in Howes, 2018a, vol. 2, 4, 112, 231.

is in real danger of being lost to the research imperatives and limiting structures of modern higher education, limitations that even the more insistent calls for interdisciplinarity cannot quite overcome (Smith, 2007b; Smith, forthcoming).

2 Languages of Feeling

The most orthodoxly historicist of our claims is the need for a renewed sensitivity to language in the archives. We discuss the importance of languages of 'feeling' in general and raise awareness of the necessity to employ historical language that transcends contemporary (universal) notions of emotion and sense. Historical concepts of experience often bear little resemblance to 'emotion' or 'sense', but rather combine affective and cognitive categories in more general concepts of feeling. We must also go beyond the word. 'Language', we argue, might usefully include the non-verbal, such as posture, expression, etc., as modes of affective bodily expression that are plausibly recoverable and historically distinct. It prompts us to suggest collapsing the usually parceled-off category of reason (mind/soul/thought/speech/brain, depending on the context) into a more inclusive category of felt experience.

In Piroska Nagy and Damien Boquet's masterful (2018) study of medieval 'sensibilities' there is a clear historicist intention to be faithful to the linguistic affective concepts of the past. This fidelity is predicated on an understanding of a relationship between concepts and experience, between concepts and expressions and between concepts and value, which is to say the moral status of affective categories. For them, the medieval European master category is *affectus*, not 'emotion' and not even passion. Indeed, the fine-grained distinction between different concepts at different times is shown to be key to understanding shifts in emotional styles and scripts, of the drawing of lines of inclusion and exclusion around otherwise loosely bound communities that share a common orientation of correct 'feeling'. In their elaborate and compelling account, Nagy and Boquet show that there can be no easy parcelling-off of emotion, sense, reason, thought, soul or virtue. Reason is an affect, in their account, and the soul's state of grace is predicated not on a simple reading of piety, but on the correct orientation and balance of the whole being. Even in these most general terms, it is, quite plainly, absurd to think of medieval pasts in terms of six basic emotions or five senses, or with a clear demarcation of reason and emotion, or of soul and body, mind and spirit. Once one folds in the intricacies of discrete affective concepts in Latin, or else in situated vernacular languages, combined with shifting interpretations of Aristotelian and Galenic traditions, and an overall narrative arc of change in the relationship of Church,

State and society over the longue durée, then one ends up looking at a distinctly alien affective totality. It is, however, anything but simple. If ever a work of history demonstrated the historical complexity of past experience, this is it.

There are similar works for antiquity and early modernity, as well as works about modern history that disrupt the canonical boundaries of psychology's recent past, so why do we still parcel them off as 'histories of emotions' or 'histories of the senses'? They quite clearly encompass both, ably representing historical experience and knowledge of experience in its own terms.[7] Unfortunately, much recent work in our respective fields fails to be so holistic, presenting a warped, one-sided and anachronistic view of the felt past.[8]

2.1 Constructing Cruelty

We cannot hope to provide a working model of how to follow situated language in all periods and places, since by definition this work will vary according to the subject matter and the availability of source material.[9] We can, however, provide an example. A fruitful line of inquiry concerns the concept, charge and experience of 'cruelty' in English from the middle of the eighteenth century through to the middle of the nineteenth century.[10] It might seem, at first blush, that cruelty, or the act of being cruel, has little to do with emotions or senses, and much to do with morals and behaviour, but the gradual development of a modern concept of cruelty in this period encapsulated all of these categories and was, to boot, laden with class and gender chauvinism and political ideology. The charge of cruelty to animals, for example, was first applied to activities and institutions – blood sports, cattle markets – in which those making the charge took no direct part. To highlight how novel the charge of cruelty was, it should be stressed that an activity like cockfighting was an ancient, high-prestige sport of the aristocracy, sharing a stage with feted

---

[7] Exemplary works include Kaster, 2005; Sullivan, 2016; Illouz, 2007.

[8] Examples here are legion. Here we highlight a few otherwise worthy works in which the problem of emotional anachronism slips in. We do not intend to condemn or de-value this scholarship in general terms. Lateiner and Spatharas, 2016; Broomhall, 2015, with the exception of chapters by Stephanie Trigg and Thomas Dixon; Bailey and Barclay, 2017, with the exception of the chapter by Helen Hills. The last referenced collection, for example, includes an attempt to establish, at the end, 'standardised . . . variables' and 'constants in biology' (Whitehouse and François, 2017). This misstep was repeated by another (otherwise excellent) collection emerging from Australia-based scholars, Kerr, Lemmings, and Phiddian, 2016, the unfitting chapter in question being Parrott, 2016.

[9] A working example of how this might look, across different periods, with a particular sensitivity to the question of translation, is Boddice, 2019c.

[10] This example is drawn from extensive familiarity with printed literature, sermons, political debates, political commentary and archival records pertaining to social activism against cruelty to animals or to the defence of traditional activities involving animals in eighteenth- and nineteenth-century Britain. This is necessarily only a sketch, but for a full account, see Boddice, 2009.

horseracing events. Bull baiting and bull running in English marketplaces went back at least as far as the thirteenth century and were connected to noble patronage. Sports like these were outlawed in 1835.[11] And the presence of livestock markets in towns and cities was ancient, the oldest (Smithfield in London) dating to the tenth century. Smithfield livestock market was closed in the 1850s.[12]

What changed was not, in the main, a moral re-framing of the status of the animal, but a moral re-framing of the behaviour of 'uncivilized' people, usually men, within the framework of emerging concepts of civilised society and the need to control what happened, including the production of smells, sounds and sights, in public and commercial spaces. The meaning of 'cruelty', therefore, first indicated a *lack of feeling*, or an insensibility, out of keeping with an age which has since been bequeathed to us as having been defined by its 'sensibility'. 'Cruelty' – 'inhumanity; savageness; barbarity', according to Johnson's (1768) *Dictionary* – was a functional synonym for 'callousness', and the two would remain interchangeable, depending on context, well into the nineteenth century. Men who engaged in cockfighting or bullbaiting, or who beat cab horses or the cattle they drove to market, were charged at first with the moral failing of feeling *nothing* with respect to their behaviour and its implications for the kind of sociability that might be expected in a civilisation where such behaviour took place. Their behaviour was described as 'brutish', which is at once to equate these men with the animals they abused and to mark their lack of sensibility. To introduce the concept of 'cruelty' into public discourse concerning these subjects and to extend the formal remit of parliamentary activity to encompass it was to do more than identify cruelty; it was to literally *construct* it. It was to say that there should be a sensibility where one presently did not exist.

This sensibility concerned both the commission of pain and the witnessing of pain, framed as a highly contingent aesthetic recipe for the sights and sounds of pain – blood and animal cries – and how to see and hear them through a new moral rubric. It therefore depended on a particularly situated concept and moral loading of the other body in pain and an extension of the kinds of bodies that could undergo this experience. It was not animal pain itself that was the moral problem to be overcome, for the dominant discourse of dominion persisted. Hardly anybody advocated giving up the slaughterhouse, the foxhunt, animal conveyance, or the wearing of fur. Rather, it was the building of a moral and sensible response to the aesthetics of such pain that was at issue, with negative judgement being preserved for those who failed to develop such a sensibility. In practice, this meant moving the appearance of animal suffering *out of sight* and out of hearing and olfactory range, with the

---

[11] For context, see Steintrager, 2004; Boddice, 2009, 81ff; Griffin, 2005.

[12] For context on the urban smellscape and market, see Henshaw, 2013, 86–93. For more general context, see Geier, 2017.

slaughterhouse and the livestock market being pushed to the urban periphery and the blood sports of the masses being barred from taking up space where those who preferred not to see it circulated. With a groundswell of opinion targeting the arenas and the markets, the people thus accused inevitably became acquainted with the charges against them, and here the concepts of cruelty and callousness can be seen slowly to diverge. For once it is known that public-opinion leaders and even legislators have scrutinised an activity and found it to be cruel/callous, pointing out the pain and suffering caused, it is no longer possible to continue that activity without first having reflected on these charges. For those on the outside, the pursuit of these activities then fell into the category of 'wanton' behaviour, where the motive for, say, fighting cocks, was said to implicitly include a pleasure in the pain caused. It was a pleasure or satisfaction experienced through the medium of a kind of anger and violence (often highlighted by the end of the eighteenth century and into the nineteenth). Johnson's (1768) definition of 'cruel' had included being 'pleased with hurting others', but Webster (1832) expanded upon it, noting the 'ferociousness' of the cruel and the 'disposition or temper' that 'gratified in giving unnecessary pain' through 'cruelty'. The charge of 'brute' was retained, but the meaning shifted from insensible (and unreasonable) animality to *unrestrained* emotional animality, a want of mercy. From inside those cultures under attack, there was anger, but it was directed at the imposition of outsiders. To continue in such activities was an act of defiance against class politics and cultural chauvinism. In any event, the men who had been first cast as insensible were now overflowing with feeling unfit for a civilised state. Cruelty in this period, at least as concerned animals, can be seen to track from an absence to a surfeit of feeling, from a lack of sympathetic reaction to the evidence of the animal body in pain to the pleasurable indulgence of causing such pain. Animality proved a flexible metaphor.

But what are we really tracking when we record this history? Throughout, it is easier to analyse this movement as a reflection of the development of the sensibility and political reach of the middle and ruling classes. It is indicative of their own intermingling of sensory, passional and moral categories, of the meaning of pain and its signs, of the intellectual understanding of human subjectivity and its aggregation in civilisation, and of their expression of this through rhetoric, social intervention in behaviour and the regulation of social space, and ultimately in the machinery of legislation. If we get beyond the intellectual and conceptual history of the making and imposition of a new category of 'cruelty', we reveal the situated history of class-based disgust or abhorrence and disdain. This history is reached obliquely, as it were, behind the charges being levelled at those deemed inferior, uncivilised, inhuman, *cruel*.[13]

---

[13] For further context, see Bourke, 2011.

Figure 1 Detail from 'The Second Stage of Cruelty', from William Hogarth's *Four Stages of Cruelty*, 1751.

The example can also be pursued in its extra-linguistic dimension, for along with the new conceptual category of cruelty came new faces of cruelty and specific postures of inhumanity. The rendering of cruel expressions is exemplary of the disgust of the sensible, for they do not depict the pleasures experienced by those said to be wanton, but rather a kind of anti-civilizational rage, an embodiment of evil: a dangerous physical sign of the animal within.

The images here, for example, which range from the mid-eighteenth century to the mid-nineteenth century, play with this horror visage atop a club-wielding body. Figure 1 is taken from the second of Hogarth's *Four Stages of Cruelty*

Figure 2 Detail from 'Am Not I A Brute and A Brother?', *Punch* (1869).

(1751) and identifies the 'inhuman wretch';[14] Figure 2 is from an 1869 issue of
Punch, with a caption that riffs on the abolitionist movement but somehow also
inverts it: 'Am not I a brute and a brother?', it reads. But who speaks, the cow or
the man? And, regardless, if the answer is 'yes', how can the situation be
redeemed? There is no humanity present, only a face to be pitied and a face to
revile. Historians of the animal protection and anti-cruelty movement regularly
employ these kinds of image, but seldom if ever have the expressions on the faces

---

[14] Boddice has focused on *The Four Stages of Cruelty* on a number of occasions, charting variously
the historical meaning of cruelty and its association with callousness and civilisation. See
Boddice, 2009, 96–102; Boddice, 2013; Boddice, 2019c, 132–42.

of those in the throes of animal torment been interpreted as oblique significations of urbane revulsion. But this is essentially *all* they can tell us.

Getting at the experience of those affected by the construction of cruelty, whether of the acceptance of the revelation of wantonness in what had been unfeeling activity, or of resistance, is much more difficult. But we can at least chart the ways in which the new moral/feeling concept was operationalised and enforced, such that even if the experience of those chiefly impacted by it is erased, we can, nevertheless, track the creation of the affective script and the ways it was gradually finessed into an affective regime. In sum, though, we see in this category of cruelty the futility of trying to parcel off emotions (an anachronism in any case) and the senses, for the language of sensibility was bound up with passions and morals and active political endeavours to re-cast what it meant to be human.

2.2 Translation

What this passage on cruelty captures is the extent to which such categories have to be rebuilt in context in order to be properly understood. The risk, ever-present, is of the easy assumption that such words and their associated moral and affective experiences are readily understood. If this is true working within the English language, an extra level of difficulty emerges when working with translations from other languages, a problem that can be extended to physical expressions and gestures, which also come laden with culturally specific meanings. The temptation with the translation of affective or feeling categories is to find words in one's own language that one assumes readers will readily understand. Thus, *caritas* becomes 'love', or *menis* becomes 'rage', to give but two popular examples.[15] The problem is that this implicitly undermines the historicism in the histories of emotions and the senses. We take seriously the conjunction of historicism, anthropology and social neuroscience on this point: that there is a fundamental relation between cultural linguistic concepts, experience and modes of expression. Concepts are formative of the meaning of affective experiences: they give those experiences their cultural and temporal particularity (Barrett, 2006a; 2006b; 2017; Boddice, 2019b; Gendron et al., 2012; Hoemann, Devlin, Barrett, 2020; Hoemann, Xu and Barrett, 2019). We cannot hope to preserve or recover those particularities if we continue to reduce them to a kind of 'core' meaning that is parlayed, however unwittingly, into universal or basic emotion systems. If we accede that feeling concepts in other languages can be readily translated into canonical contemporary psychological categories

---

[15] See Rosenwein, 2016, 22, 55, 87, 96, 158 for a range of contextualised meanings of *caritas*; for the treatment of *menis* see Boddice, 2019c, 21–9.

in English then the whole purpose of historicising them goes up in smoke. There seems to be an almost irresistible temptation to perform this kind of translation, to say that medieval *affectus* or *passio* is what 'we' mean by 'emotion', or that eighteenth-century sympathy is what 'we' call 'empathy', or that, essentially, whatever label we choose, we are talking about *emotion*.[16] Even when scholars go through the motions of adding subtextual caveats acknowledging the short-comings of translating, say, *eudaemonia* into 'happiness', or worse, 'well-being', they nevertheless *do it anyway*.[17] It creates an epistemological slippage that, even with the best of intentions, prevents historical or culturally relative understanding. The solution, inconvenient as it may seem, is to treat such categories on their own terms, to explicate them through a thorough understanding of the context in which they were used and to avoid shorthand translation. If this makes our historical works more difficult to research, to write and to read, then so be it. We submit that the histories of emotions and the senses are not supposed to be easy, for they push against one of the most fundamental and unquestioned phenomenological assumptions of our own lives, namely, that how *we* feel must be how *other* people felt.

2.3 Convergence

The problem, summed up, seems rather prosaic. The success of this or that study seems to rest on the extent to which its primary identification as a 'history of emotions' or a 'history of the senses' is understood to be an invitation to disrupt easy or canonical (and contemporary) definitions. Those that enter uncritically into the field tend to reproduce psychological reductions and essentialisms. Might we find a way to avoid such problems? Aside from the obvious deficiency that we have two fields – emotions and senses – when we perhaps ought to have only one, the combination of those two fields presents us more concretely with the problem of overcoming these discrete and distinctly modern languages of feeling, sensibility and sensation. A combination of our efforts would be of little value if, in practice, we still ended up talking about emotions here and senses there. It is not simply that their entanglement is so plain in so many contexts, but that the very notion of *entanglement* recapitulates emotions and senses as discrete categories and risks blinding us to the situated conceptualisation and experience of affective life.

---

[16] There are numerous examples of this kind of conceptual latitude among scholars who are otherwise extremely precise about language choice. See Rosenwein, 2016, 7–8, 17; Plamper, 2015, 12, 299; Frevert, 2011, 12; Eustace, 2008, 3, 76–7.

[17] An entire academic industry is built upon this. For a review, see Boddice, 2019c, 45–7, 169–87; for a critical take on positive psychology more generally, see Cabanas and Illouz, 2019.

The solution we present, and which will occupy the rest of this Element, is a shift towards precisely this category of 'experience'. To make this shift, we have to make it perfectly clear what we do not mean by this: a subject we take up in the next section through the lens of Joan Scott in particular. But it seems important at this juncture also to make sure that we jettison another potential source of misdirection: intellectual history. Intellectual history is vital to a situated history of linguistic concepts, but we must take care that it does not entirely supplant the kinds of experiential projects that we wish to produce. To put this in crude terms, a history of emotions cannot properly call itself such if it fails to connect ideas about what emotions are and how they work to how they feel in practice. Lines have to be drawn that connect ideas to experience, predicated on an understanding that the production of cultural scripts both springs from and impacts upon embodied and embrained realities. To that end, we want to discount any notion that a history of experience is purely about the word 'experience' and its situated usage. What we propose incorporates this, to be sure, but we prefer here to use the word 'experience' in the abstract. This concept does not need to be alive in a given historical context in order for us to take an analytical position regarding the experience of historical actors. We attach no hidebound definition to the word and, moreover, release it from its own past as a fairly regular feature in the history of ideas. By experience we mean, simply, to capture the lived, meaningful reality of historical actors, whether as subjective or collective reality, and incorporating all the features of past perception in their own terms, be they sensory, emotional, cognitive, supernatural or whatever. We might have used the language of 'feeling' to attain a similar position, since in English usage this word has the capacity to conflate or confuse the senses, the emotions and intentional thought, but on reflection the category of experience seems to be even more flexible. It permits all elements of lived reality, including such things that might not readily be appreciated as factors in how life feels, from homeostasis to political orientation. It forces us to appreciate and to reconstruct historical context in the broadest possible terms and in the most nimble of forms, in order to provide access to the historical traces left to us, be they verbal or gestural or symbolic, that pertain to discrete experiences of reality.

While on the one hand this must concentrate our attention on what historical actors precisely mean by the words they record, and to take supreme care in the act of translation not to superimpose contemporary interpretations of reality over historical ones, on the other hand we must remain alive to the non-verbal, and to the body and the brain.

3 Towards Experience

In this section we illustrate how recent work in our respective fields would benefit from critical collaboration, recapitulating the value of interdisciplinary work, bridging cultural anthropology, history and social neuroscience. We also discuss examples of scholarship that already are clearly heading in the right direction, even if they lack a coherent or comprehensive theoretical framework. We evaluate the re-entanglement of emotions and senses, mind and body, which propels us towards a fuller, more textured understanding of practices of being human. In pointing the way forward, and building on the aforementioned points, we recapitulate the need for a radical overhaul of certain attractive but untenable universalising emphases that privilege the 'natural' in human bodies at the level of sense and affect. Our collapsing of the categories of emotions and senses, with interdisciplinary collaboration, ought to equip us much more substantially to carry this out.

We approach the question, 'what is the new history of experience?' through a negative construction, by addressing the inescapable Joan Scott (1991). Her 1991 article is a valuable piece of important criticism, at the core of which is the right idea, the right impetus and an appropriate warning. Scott's major criticism of those who fell back on the 'evidence of experience' was that experience was treated as foundational, irreducible. It was grounded in something universal, something fundamental, something that could not be gainsaid or deconstructed. As such, Scott argued, its use only served to further highlight the power structures that drew lines of social exclusion, never getting at the how of experience's situated construction: 'The evidence of experience then becomes evidence for the fact of difference, rather than a way of exploring how difference is established, how it operates, how and in what ways it constitutes subjects who see and act in the world . . . . the evidence of experience . . . reproduces rather than contests given ideological systems' (777–8). In Scott's terms, this 'experience' was constituted by things like 'desire, homosexuality, heterosexuality, femininity, masculinity, sex, and even sexual practices', which were treated by historians as given, natural, ahistorical categories that objectively existed below the level of discourse, providing a backstop against the untrammelled imagination of the post-modern scholar. She was having none of it (778). All those categories, she said, ought themselves to be subject to historicism. There was nothing natural or foundational about experience. To accept it as such was actually to partake uncritically and unreflectively in making invisible the forces that drew lines of exclusion.

Early on in the paper, Scott begins to unfold her notion of what was required to rectify the situation. We need, she wrote, 'to attend to the historical processes that, through discourse, position subjects and produce their experiences'.

Experience was to be defined by 'that which we seek to explain, that about which knowledge is produced. To think about experience in this way is to historicize it as well as to historicize the identities it produces' (779–80). She asked whether history could 'exist without foundations and what it might look like if it did' (781). The problem – a problem unseeable in 1991 – is the utter abandonment of the body. Scott, in all her criticism of historians who fell back upon foundations to rationalize their histories, in turn fell back on discourse as the root of everything. Discourse may itself have been subject to change over time, but it was the shaping force nonetheless, the ultimate foundation. Human formation and experience were not possible to conceive without it.

Scott's abandonment of the body was conscious, deliberate. She criticized those who turned to 'feelings' or the 'sensuous' because those who did so assumed that these categories represented realities that could not be 'subsumed by "language"', a so-called 'prediscursive reality directly felt, seen, and known'. They were fundamentally ahistorical, used to grant insight and authenticity, for example, to the woman historian writing women's history because there was an attribute to the category 'woman' that held true over time, a foundational connection (786–7). Experience, on these terms, 'establishes a realm of reality outside of discourse and it authorizes the historian who has access to it' (790). She insisted that 'experience is a linguistic event' that is not 'confined to a fixed order of meaning' (793). Scott was unable to see how to include the body and the brain, the feelings and the senses, unable to see beyond discourse, while retaining a grip on the historicisation of everything. These problems now seem surmountable, and Scott was on to something, from the point of view of historiographical intent. She wanted to understand the 'processes by which identities are ascribed, resisted, or embraced', but she assumed these processes to be 'discursive' only. She wanted to take 'all categories of analysis as contextual, contested, and contingent', but could not work out how this could apply to the brain/body, so dismissed it (796). The new history of experience shares the desire to treat 'the emergence of concepts and identities as historical events in need of explanation', but it does not any longer assume that it can do this within the realm of language alone (792). Yes, the 'history of these concepts ... becomes the evidence by which "experience" can be grasped and by which the historian's relationship to the past he or she writes about can be articulated', but we no longer presume to isolate conceptual history from the history of the brain, from the history of emotions and/or senses, from the history of the body, from the history of interoception, from the history of epigenetic and microevolutionary adaptations, from the knowledge about biological, neurological plasticity (796). Scott left off by 'insisting on the discursive nature of "experience" and on the politics of its construction' (797), but we cannot help flag the contradiction in her language use here: the discursive was natural, foundational, just the kind of thing she was decrying in others. We also cannot help pointing out that Scott had no evidence that experience, as she wished to define it, was entirely discursively constituted. It was an expression of the postmodern moment, which claimed for the discursive master category no further proof, only further deconstructive practice.[18] As Paul Stenner (2017, 207) has put it, acerbically, 'This kind of analysis is all very well – indeed it was admirable in an historical context where most of psychology studiously excluded everyday discourse as methodological noise – but meanwhile, the windows and doors tend to get shut to whatever is not discourse'.

We do not know where Scott currently stands on the evidence of experience and perhaps it does not matter. We address her article because it remains on the lips of those who took from it an impression that the history of experience was actually impossible. As post-modernism imploded, what was left in Scott's piece was the criticism of those historians who fell back on natural or universal qualities of the human, and that criticism remains valid. The history of emotions and the history of the senses, as those fields have developed over the last three decades, have witnessed their fair share of research which remains in thrall to a kind of biological reduction, an overly determined take on human beings that assumes something 'basic', transcendent, automatic, a-cultural. It was this that Roger Cooter (in press) excoriated when he talked of a new dark age, descending as the humanities abandoned themselves to evolutionary biology, where the meaning of being human was surrendered to the affect theorists. We too criticize this kind of work, and surely Scott must hate it on the same terms, as being purely additive. It does nothing to historicise the categories it conjures with, be it love or touch or fear or smell, but simply talks about love or touch or fear or smell in a given context, as if love or touch or fear or smell are simply self-evident, readily accessibly affects, accessible because in the final analysis we are all human.

The better work in the history of emotions and the history of the senses has rejected this approach, not out of hand, but through substantial empirical work that has demonstrated the historicity of 'emotions' and 'senses', the whole affective apparatus of the human and its corresponding array of experiences. Some of us, too, have been alive to the developments across the disciplinary boundary, especially in social psychology (or the psychosocial) and the social

---

[18] We are far from being the first to make this point (see, for example, Kounine, 2018, 12–13; Hinton, 2011, 19), but the re-turn to the body and the brain as sites of historicism, as plastic objects in dynamic relation with the world, with culture, practice and discourse, requires an understanding of bodily potential and limits. It is one thing to invoke the body and the brain, but if we then fail to instantiate bodies and brains and what they do we shall be no better off than the social neuroscientist who invokes culture and then fails to investigate culture's implications.

neurosciences. Most important here is research that connects conceptual development to brain development, conjoining a cultural plasticity to a neurological plasticity, to make a bioculturally dynamic gestalt out of the human being. Scott could not have foreseen this. We want to emphasise most strongly that this is not simply a case of culture writing to nature (Boddice, 2018a, 143; cf. Smail, 2008). That would essentialise the dualism once again, preserving base and superstructure, as it were, and give preference to the primacy of discourse favoured by Scott in 1991. No, on the contrary, this work has shown the extent to which conceptual development alters brains, but it must also account for the extent to which brains impact the conceptual field. The brain–body and the world have become entwined in a dynamic of cause and effect that helps explain not only the historicity of language, but the historicity of the human itself. This is the history without foundation about which Scott dreamed. We doubt she would have countenanced putting the brain–body back in the frame in order to fulfil it.

To be clear, then, what we are proposing is a development of the interface of history with neuroscience, but in such a way that rejects any recourse to the kind of foundations that Scott decried back in the early 90s. We expand upon this in the next two sections. Elsewhere Boddice (2018b) and others (McGrath, 2017; Burman, 2012, 2014) have tried to show where Daniel Lord Smail's (2008) 'neurohistory' project made its missteps, and how Lynn Hunt's (2009) shallow recourse to affect theory oversimplified our potential to access the experience of the past. Both these scholars, and especially Smail, did wonders for historians looking to overcome a disciplinary hurdle, but both ultimately surrendered to the other discipline, holding to the universal, the basic, the transcendent to undergird the contingent, the mutable, the historical. Likewise, when presenting this criticism to the remarkably open community of transcultural psychiatrists in Montreal – a group dead set on acknowledging the role of culture in the making of brains – it was met with a gentle but determined request to soft-pedal the historicism, to allow some kind of universal substrate of humanness, some recourse to things that need of no inquiry because we all already implicitly know.[19] In return, we might complain that a ready willingness to see the same in humans in all times in all places actively prevents us from seeing the differences. When the desire to see sameness is stated at the outset, it is wishful thinking, unless that sameness can be demonstrated instead of simply being asserted. So far, it seems to us, all attempts to demonstrate it, especially among psychologists and evolutionary biologists, have been assertions in scientific

---

[19] Their own contribution to the biocultural view should not be overlooked. See Choudhury and Kirmayer, 2009, and Kirmayer and Crafa, 2014.

garb, methodologically flawed political manoeuvres that are expressive of an institutionalised orthodoxy, and, so far, the practitioners of this 'science' have not answered, by any measure of satisfaction, the criticisms levelled at them by the likes of Ruth Leys (2017). And to be clear, historicism does not, in the place of a priori continuity, substitute a priori change. Rather, it assumes nothing in advance. While we are inevitably constructive in our historical narratives and political in our selections, we are nonetheless guided principally by what we find (pace Hayden White, 1974). The trick, it seems to us, is to be properly configured to the process of finding, which is to say, free from a priori assumptions about what the affective past might throw up.

We are, then, following Scott in the rejection of foundations, in the historicisation of experience itself, but we are rejecting her own foundations. Necessarily, we are also moving on from the history of emotions and the senses as analytically discrete categories, combining them to explore experience more broadly. The new history of experience, which we have here presented via a critical reading of Joan Scott, but which is meant to be sympathetic to Scott's critical bent, is designed to address a bigger question than the history of emotions or senses seem fit either to ask or to answer by themselves.

3.1 Definition?

In promoting a new history of experience there will be an immediate demand for definition, and the focus will be on the word 'experience'. There is a semantic minefield, which, though extensively picked over by historians and philosophers, as well as physiologists and anthropologists, is still packed with explosives. Does the history of 'experience' simply have to do all over again what historians of emotions have had to go through with 'emotion', with them defending multivalent definitions and analytical distance, while others bombard them with fixed meanings? What to do? First, it bears mentioning that by focusing on 'experience' we do not, as with 'emotions', pit ourselves against the psychological behemoth of funding and institutionalisation, with all of its spillover into popular culture, such that we have to do battle with the lay public's common sense. By shifting focus, we can leverage our attack on that behemoth by demonstrating its limited vision. More important, however, is our need constantly to assert the principle of historicism, over and above any attachment to a particular category of analysis. 'Experience', therefore, is a label that gives us an analytical place to stand, but we should not mean anything by it in an a priori sense. We are after how it felt, or how it was, to the historical actor, defined by whatever notion of the self or the subject or the collective was in play for the actor in question at the time. This does not lead us to a contextualised discussion of 'experience' in history, but to the ways in which living was real in historical terms. We think there is an opportunity here to offer a radical new interpretation of Ranke's vision of history *wie es eigentlich gewesen ist*, where the *eigentlich* is not tested or verified against the trope of philosophical reason, but rather becomes interesting as a perception of reality that is lived as if that perception was real. From this 'as if' stem action, interaction, practice, sensation, feeling, 'emotion', thought, and so on. The situated *eigentlich* becomes causative, irrespective of what a more traditional account of 'objective' reality might suggest. When Plato (2000, book 6) critiqued opinion (*eikasia*) and belief (*pistis*), those things that seem to be true, as being inferior forms of knowledge to thought (*dianoia*) and true understanding (*noesis*), he nevertheless emphasised for us (book 7) that the people in bonded slavery in the cave who saw shadows on the wall, caused by a fire, lived this experience as if it were real, and as if it were all there was. He was, of course, suggesting a route out of such delusion, away from the sensory perception of reality towards a 'true' understanding of reality, but the historian's attention reverts to the question of what it would be like to think the shadows were the objects that made them, that the fire was the sun, and so on. What do people do on the basis of life as it actually is to them, in Plato's terms, as they believe it to be, in the context of meaning-making in which perception is situated? Not 'actually is' to any other standard of empirical verification, but only as it is to them (which can, of course, include a perception of the value of empirical verification, but this too must be situated).

There is also an ethics to this contextualized understanding of human experience. Put simply, even clumsily: can historical experience be consumed, used, and even monetized in the present? If it can, should it? We believe not only that it cannot but that precisely because it is impossible to re-experience with fidelity the way people in the past experienced their sensory and emotional worlds we are (happily) saved from the ethical missteps of the enterprise. While, for example, re-enactors of wars, recreators of historical sites, and curators of living museums ardently and enthusiastically invite us to re-experience the past as it was lived, our framing here of historical experience makes it quite clear that such invitations are (mercifully) bereft of the mechanisms needed to achieve these goals. Not only can we not reproduce the sensory and emotional signatures of a given time and place; we are simply ill-equipped to re-consume them, re-experience them in the same way that contemporaries did (Smith, 2007a; 2015a). Despite earnest and well-meaning calls to, for example, re-live the stench, sights, sounds, tastes and touches of battle, war, conflict and strife, the understanding of human historical experience we offer here reveals not only the ontological impossibility of such efforts but the ethical undesirability of them. There is a reason, after all, war re-enactors do not re-enact the

Holocaust. Efforts to re-experience the past in this way are exclusively modern conceits and our approach exposes the flimsy logic of our own historical moment (Smith, 2015).

This approach goes against the grain of the common perception that we can and do readily experience the past. To be consistent, we must reconcile our conviction to put trust in subjective perception as reality with our resistance to re-experiencing the past in historiographical practice. After all, memorialisation is specifically designed to make the past present, either as a spark of individual, subjective memory, or to provide historical insight through the medium of experience to those who were not present at the historical moment in question. Here we must make a crucial distinction, between the historical moment and its memory, and an observation about the plasticity of subjective experience itself. To the historical actor, the experience of an 'event' is often tied to a discrete moment or period in time, but the experience itself has the potential to change through the activity of memory, which is filtered by the process of time, new information, lost information, new conditions, and so on. To this extent, the experience of an event *lives*, and we might straightforwardly extend this observation to the experience of the past through memorialisation. To visit a former Nazi concentration camp, or a Stasi prison, or museum of slavery, or indeed any site explicitly designed to keep the memory of a past alive, visitors subjectively and collectively experience the past through the medium of the present but, and this is key, they do not re-experience the past, despite implicit and explicit curatorial invitations to do so. Insofar as, for example, suffering is evoked, memorialisation does not recreate the original suffering, but refracts it. An experience can be guided, shaped by didactic strategies to ensure that the lived experience conforms to the prescribed experience. What we want to emphasise is that historians, who are no less subject to such refracted experiences than anyone else, need to find a way to bracket this kind of experience in historical writing, for it is in no way informative of the situated historical experience of the place or time being memorialised. Since historians do play an important role in the making of memorialisations, it is incumbent upon them to represent the distance between the lived experience thus 'remembered' and the lived experience of those who *visit* that memory. Indeed, this particular mode of experiencing history is subject to academic scrutiny in its own right, and forms a field separate to that which we pursue here (Brauer and Lücke, 2013).[20]

---

[20] The field of history and memory is vast, and we touch here only lightly upon it. For a recent assessment of the stakes in this field, see Cubitt, 2014.

None of this is meant to suggest that historic sites and living museums cannot serve as effective communicators or even custodians of the past; but it does mean that they need to be transparent and open when doing so. Quietly piping sounds and smells into museum spaces without explicit commentary on what those lived in the past thought of those smells and sounds, the context-specific meaning they attached to them, is tantamount to playing a sensory and emotional shell game not only with unwitting visitors but with history itself. As Robert Jütte has noted, using the senses can be profitable for museums; some make good money on selling the past through the senses (Jütte 2005, 1–9). But tremendous care needs to be taken here. Catering to contemporary appetites for 'authentic' historical experience, reinforcing nostalgic conceits (emotional and sensory), and inviting patrons to experience the past in the present is rife with problems. Careful contextualisation can go a long way to correcting them even if the forms of contextualisation are not especially seductive or exciting. Traditional print (brochures, written explanations) can perform important work here and allow visitors to understand the historically situated meanings of the senses and, indeed, emotions, museums often enthusiastically deploy (Bijsterveld, 2015; Smith, 2015).

All of this takes us – we think with a clean break – away from former attempts at the history of experience, as well as from the intellectual, rhetorical and etymological history of 'experience' that was definitive of, for example, Martin Jay's (2006) *Songs of Experience*. We have addressed Scott already, but it should not have escaped anyone that our approach to experience is a complete upheaval and a polar opposite of those Scott had in her sights, explicitly or implicitly. Experience as a universal, or as limited to individual subjectivity, or as foundational, or as purely rational, as in the frameworks of Dilthey (2002) and Collingwood (1946; Dray, 1995; Jay, 2006, 216–60), is rejected. The historian can neither re-experience nor re-enact the past, but only reconstruct it as far as is possible.[21] Where these historians sought a foundation in something transcendent and held in common, simply waiting for the correctly and mystically attuned historian, we set ourselves free from foundations, including that of discourse in the work of Scott and the neurobiological reductionism of certain sciences. Here we take a more radical position than those who have argued for the historicisation of subjectivity, in which the history of emotions (and presumably the senses) are said to be rooted. To subject the concept of 'self' to historicism must entail the possibility that 'subjectivity' is not experienced as such. Inter-subjective or collective formation, or some other type of formation, are conceivable as processes of experience, such that the terms

---

[21] As such, we are at some distance from phenomenological accounts such as Carr, 2014.

'subjective', 'self', 'person', 'psyche', 'agency' and 'I' are themselves revealed to be universalising foundations.[22]

Meanwhile, such a work as Jay's ought really be a last word on 'experience' as an historical category in its own right. Through its highlighting of the high stakes of the meaning and value of 'experience' over the longue durée, it is of tremendous importance, but it is not, ultimately, exemplary of what we are trying to do, even if at times we overlap with its material. Occasionally, Jay takes us to the brink of a history of experience as we are trying to frame it, but he pulls away in the quest for situated definitions – the idea of experience – instead of pursuing historical experiences or lived experiences in their own right. See, for example, Jay's (2006, 27) reading of Montaigne's 'Of Experience', where he strives to understand what Montaigne understood by the word, when the work discussed leads irrevocably to the phenomenon itself, to the 'lived reality' of the inhabitation of a human body. One of us (Boddice, 2016; 2021; 2022) has dealt and continues to deal with material related to the age of experimental science at the end of the nineteenth and beginning of the twentieth century, where the words 'experience', 'experiment' and 'expertise' are constantly in play. An intellectual-historical account of them would not be at all out of place in Jay's work, but we would be interested in them only insofar as they provide partial access to how it felt to practice experimental science at the time. We can reiterate, for what it is worth, that most established medical scientists by 1900 understood that there was no substitute for direct experience, for the repetition of experiments, for the learning of physiological facts. No book would serve as a viable proxy. But that does not get at what it was like to follow through on such principles. It remains to be asked, what was the actual experience of a belief in the value of 'experience'? And while the situated concept of 'experience' will play a part in the answer to this question, it will be but a part of a broader approach that seeks to understand how it was, actually, to attain and produce knowledge in this manner.

3.2 The Perils of Empathy

Coming back to Joan Scott, her chief criticism of the category of experience was that it privileged the historian's own experience as, say, 'woman', in order to be able to divine the experience of women in the past. As we have already argued, the rejection of anything universal or biologically essential ought to be one step in removing this danger of the uncritical transference

---

[22] As a helpful guide, see Eustace, 2008, chapters on love and anger in particular. See Kounine, 2018, 13–20, for an example of the tensions that are introduced when the stated method includes such foundations but the historical situation tends to suggest their rejection.

of the historian's personal and unchecked experience into the past. But it is not in itself sufficient. There has, also, to be a conscious process of self-examination in order to understand our own politics of selection, attention, preference, exclusion, selfhood, time and place. While we may ask *where?* and *when?* we must do so with an acknowledgement that in the process of reconstructing a period and a place we have already imposed the concepts of 'period' and 'place' on our material, such that we can view it through a particular lens of a 'there' and a 'then'. The analytical strategies we use as historians to distance ourselves from our material cannot remain invisible, perhaps because they are unavoidable. Processes of reconstruction are not neutral, even in our best efforts at allowing historical actors to speak, to sense, to feel. Yet partiality should not put us off. Nicole Eustace (2008) in particular has shown how productive it can be to self-consciously shed contemporary conceptions of the self conceived as an individual in order the better to see selves constructed differently (as a social collective, say) in the past. While this is primarily about the practice of history, it cannot help but reveal our own moment in time, illuminating the constructedness of our own perceptions of naturalness. In essence, we are suggesting that historians must build an extra step into their research, in which their own apparently automatic reactions to their sources are consciously considered and cast aside from their historical analysis.[23]

If this sounds like an Evans-like defence of historical method, we shall wear it. But we think it actually goes further than Evans (1997), taking to task not only the discourse-centred doyens of post-modernist historiography, but the ancients of empiricism as well. For while Scott (1991) couldn't see past discourse to the mutability of biology, and Hayden White (1973) missed the situated emotions in his sources because they were made to serve the universalism of the plot device (Boddice, 2018a, 15–18), empirical research with its faith in finding and recovering some truth in the archives has unwittingly imposed a universal human into its analyses.[24] The most fundamental

---

[23] Tyson Retz (2018, 218) has suggested that 'empathetic inquiry in history should direct itself towards a specific kind of context – the context in which it was possible for past agents to hold their beliefs as true and to act upon them accordingly', but notes that the usage of 'empathy' in this context might still be 'deceptive'. In intent, Retz certainly shares much with our project set forth here, but we should rather consciously abandon empathy, while forcing a critical awareness of implicit tendencies to *feel with* historical actors. We must acknowledge and make explicit where this is happening in order to be able properly to see historical contexts in their own terms. See also Davis, Jr., 2001, 3. Davis and others refused to abandon 'empathy' because it was 'too valuable', but we rate it overvalued, obscure not just for readers of history, but clearly also for practitioners and teachers.

[24] It would be impossible to demonstrate the extent of this, but it is exemplified by the transmogrification of the historical human and its *thing* in Thucydides' historiographical opening to *The*

assumption in historiography writ large is that we know what *we* are, irrespective of a growing self-consciousness about the politics of the category 'we'. Thus, we return to Scott and go further. It is not only historians who appeal to the evidence of their own experience who are making a critical error. It is all historians who do this implicitly. The appeal to the evidence of experience runs like a red thread through a great bulk of recent historiography, hidden in plain sight by virtue of being unsaid, and this is far more dangerous, to our minds, than those who explicitly appeal to the 'evidence of experience'. It supplies a kind of authority and an implicit appeal to authenticity, of which neither stand much scrutiny.

If, as more critical historians of the senses and the emotions have argued, things like disgust, anger, fear, sympathy, empathy, and so on, are historically specific and contingent, then our own sensory and emotional reaction to the historical material we encounter cannot be permitted to be formative of historical analysis.[25] We must own, explicitly, those reactions and try to understand them in their own historical and political particularities, because they are unlikely to help us reach the experience of the past, even when it seems apparently close to us.

This last caveat merits closer attention. There is an unsurprising assumption that our capacity to know, to reconstruct, the experience of the past becomes more difficult the further removed we are from our own time. In some respects this is simply true, especially where we have a small source base that reflects the lives of only a small section of society. Yet this has been true of *all* historical projects, and we have long since learnt to acknowledge the fragmentary nature of the knowledge we can produce. Moreover, this is true of *all* historical periods, in some cases because there are simply too many sources rather than too few. It bears repeating, however, that we make a grave error if we assume an as-it-were *natural* understanding of the experience of the past, simply because a certain past is close to us in time. This is to underestimate the extent to which conceptual, bodily,

---

Peloponnesian War by a raft of English translators after Hobbes. In almost every case, this ambiguous entity is reduced to a transhistorical universal, captured by the phrase 'human nature'. For a critique, see Boddice, 2019c, 35–43.

[25] It is quite common for historians to assume the meaning of 'empathy' and to assume that their readers also know what this term means, but it is far from stable as a concept and no less fixed as an experience. There are two historiographical threads here that can only be hinted at: 1. Concerning the casual employment of empathy in historical writing, and 2. Concerning the history and critical study of the concept and experience of empathy. To this should also be added, 3. Similar critical divisions in other disciplines where empathy is either understood a priori to be an objectively measurable quality that is understood in fixed terms, and 4. Empathy understood as a plastic concept, open to challenge and reappraisal. For 1, see, for example, Lydon, 2020; Carrera, 2014; for 2, see Winter, 2016; Lanzoni, 2018; for 3, a prominent example is Bloom, 2017; for 4, see Young, 2012.

cultural and political change can occur with acute rapidity, and to overestimate the extent to which our own implicit understanding of the human condition is somehow good enough to make sense of how past actors felt. Again, the assumption that we understand our own experience well enough, without serious examination of the webs in which we are caught, to be able to apply it to *any* past, is a conceit that emotional and sensory historicism ought to have shattered. If this assumption goes unchecked, then historical reconstruction is nothing more than temporal colonialism or archival ventriloquism. We have to do and be better than this.

Insofar as this position aims at an analytical perspective as if 'from nowhere', it carries with it none of the universalising baggage that ran through various romances of objectivity. Rather, it assumes nothing a priori about the experiences of past actors, whether distant from us in time and place, or whether temporally near. Continuity and similarity are not ruled out by this but have to be discovered and documented to the same extent that change and unfamiliarity have to be contextualised and explicated. It has been put to us that, whatever we do, there will always be a process and a politics of selection, of framing, of focus, of interest. It has been put to us, also, that however we recast the human as part of a world–body–brain dynamic, any history written according to this premise is still a discursive act. While we explore the context of possibilities (see Section 5) of past actors in terms of their own navigation of their space of experience and an historical horizon of expectation, to put it in Koselleck's (2002) terms, we nonetheless deal in our own, conceptually situated space, with its own horizon of expectation. The very questions we ask of the past are products of a particular present, and they are personal and partial and historical in invisible ways. We are, in claiming to cast off empathy, nonetheless disingenuously covering the tracks of our real presence and conceptual framing in the narratives of the past that we are constructing. We shall admit an unavoidable partiality – both of what we can find and of how we might tell of it – but we do not call it a limitation, much less a fatal flaw. The abdication of universality removes the connection of *our* experience to the experience of the past, and this is the crucial historiographical break. If we ask, simply, how *was* it, or how did it *feel*, to be there, then, then the politics of selection pertain to the specific there and then chosen for analysis, as well as to the conceptual specificity of 'period' or 'place'. To that extent, our approach is mitigated in the same way as *all* historical approaches, and the problem seems intractable. To jettison an assumption of familiarity, or of the capacity for empathy, might itself suggest new avenues of historical inquiry and new foci, and to that extent we acknowledge that the histories produced under this framework might very well be products of its own situated historiographical framework. But all of this will be no less subject to scrutiny, augmentation and revision than in any other historical field. The things we cannot see or examine in ourselves that nonetheless guide us in our historical research will, in due course, become the research material for future historians of experience who will ask, perhaps, 'how was it to be an historian of experience in 2020?'

4 Beings Human

Emotions and sensory history share a common interest in how being human has been meaningfully experienced, and we reassert that herein lies the value of historical enquiry. We argue that an artificial division between emotions and senses, and a tendency to employ presentist and highly problematic definitions of those two terms, actually stands in the way of understanding the human as an historical and biocultural entity. This section draws together threads from different disciplines, with particular attention paid to the biocultural model currently sending shockwaves through the psychology community writ large, and which is sure to develop further. We implore historians to take seriously these developments, new and old, and examine their implications for some principal categories of analysis, many of which collapse. Specifically, it may no longer be useful or justifiable to think in terms of emotions, senses and even cognition (or mind, or soul) as discrete elements of human experience, but rather to see them all as culturally contingent and dynamically connected parts of a whole. At the same time, we outline how an openness to such a collapse can make history a necessary contributor to emotion and sensory science, beyond the realm of the humanities, since historical data largely supports social neuroscientific and cultural anthropological claims. Not infrequently, carefully contextualised historical research serves to help refine the science. In general, historians have borrowed at will from other disciplines; we aim to lend something in return. Necessarily, such claims and aims require a reflection on methodology and application.

The specific inspiration for the critical stance here was aroused by a reading of Hannah Newton's 2018 book *Misery to Mirth: Recovery from Illness in Early Modern England*, but we want to dispel any thought that we are singling Newton out. There are many works that do the same kind of methodological hand-wringing that Newton's does, but Newton's book has the singular advantage of attempting to discuss the history of the emotions and the history of the senses, in order to arrive at a history of experience. That is, more or less, the trajectory we want to take, so it is particularly useful for us to pivot around. And while we're going to stress where we find problems with Newton's swift dealing with the methodological issues here, we want to preface this criticism with the observation that in practice the book turns out very well, which is reflective of the old trope that historians are much better at doing history then they are about talking about doing history.

Newton ultimately arrives at a position in which the declarations left in archival traces are taken seriously and literally, with an understanding that in order to do both one first has to reconstruct the context – both linguistic and cultural – lest the words are misunderstood. Monique Scheer (2012), as for so many others, comes to rescue a situation that might otherwise seem hopeless, collapsing the gap between the formalities of expression and the experience of the situation through practice theory. This is how the book plays out, most satisfactorily. Yet something lingers in the methodological discussion that disquiets. For the passage that ends with this resolution begins with 'the difficulty of accessing authentic experience', of 'disentangling sincere feelings from conventional formulae' (Newton, 2018, 28). Despite Newton's resolution of precisely this in the work of Scheer, her note that 'on reflection' this injection of 'a dose of optimism' about the possibility of gaining 'insights into past feelings', is hardly a resolute statement of methodological confidence (30). The notion of a gap between prescription and authenticity is raised as if these things might both exist as discrete categories. While they remain entangled in the archival traces, and in the practice of the writing of history, the implication is that the historical actor's actual lived experience would have included an awareness of the limited penetration of prescription, beyond which lay how she *really* felt. And this *authentic* feeling lies out of reach for us. Despite the equivocation, half of Newton's book is about 'personal experiences' (93ff), with a reassurance at the beginning of that section that the 'methodological challenges of accessing sensory and emotional experiences have been discussed in the Introduction, and so will not be repeated here' (98). Discussed, yes, briefly, but hardly resolved. We cannot shake the methodological aporia. What's more, aside from a few experienced historians of emotions and senses, we would say this is characteristic of the field at large.

The whole notion of authenticity, as something untouched by culture, something fundamentally human, something *basic*, should be cast aside. The language of authenticity has a place if we understand it, in William Reddy's terms, as emotive success: of the matching of inward feeling and contextualised expectations for expression, but even then there remains a risk that we keep alive the epistemological possibility of isolating the inward feeling from its cultural situation. There simply is no recourse to this *pure* feeling, to this reduced human mechanism. Show us a human outside of culture and we will show you something that is not human at all. One might perform an introspective exercise. Can I separate out my 'authentic experience' from 'conventional formulae'? Can I dig deep into myself and discover how I *really* feel, at any given moment, with complete disregard for the modes of expression in which I am situated, including gestural, linguistic, conceptual and interpersonal categories? To abandon all of this, even were it possible, would be to rob oneself of the very framework for understanding what one is living. If we cannot do it for ourselves, why should this be raised for historical actors? As Chris Millard (2020, 194) has put it, 'our most private inner life, our most potent experiences are always already parsed, structured and interpreted' in 'vast intellectual and practical ways' and, we should add, through processes of situated biocultural development and growth.[26]

Others might answer that, if introspection is not the way, perhaps *real* experience can be derived objectively, by machines that can literally see or measure what is going on inside and out. If it were possible, it too would largely rule out the history of experience, since being alive would be a precondition of measurement. But the things we can thus measure do not grant access to experience by themselves. The analysis of behaviour does not capture emotional experience any more than the measurement of physiological responses to stimulation captures sensory experience; cortisol is not stress; lights in the brain are not intrinsically meaningful; adrenalin is not fear, and so on. This is why we focus here on experience as it is *lived*, for the meaning of whatever is happening to the body, and the meaning of whatever the brain does either as a reaction to stimulus or as a constructive or predictive process, is done in a place, in a time, in a context, all of which are irrevocably bound with both the individual's own experience (what they have *undergone* in their lives) and the cultural framework through which that experience is made meaningful. The *lived* experience happens only in this situated way, but it also contributes to the situation in a way that keeps it more or less unstable. If history reveals anything fundamental about the human being it is that this entity and the collectives in which it lives are anything but static. Change over time applies not only to institutions and to discourse. The biocultural human is imbricated in these institutions and discourses, and is therefore also subject to change – change at the level of how it feels *to be* – on a temporal scale that does not require evolutionary biology to justify it. Without wishing to be too grand about this, history can provide responses to the question, 'What is the meaning of life?', and the responses are *when*? and *where*? and *who*? Once these parameters are narrowed down, we might even approach an answer to the question. Authenticity will not feature unless it is acknowledged that all lived experience is authentic to the person who lived it.[27]

---

[26] Millard in turn is building on an argument by Shortall, 2014, 205–6.

[27] For an account of authenticity as a political concept, see Umbach and Humphrey, 2018.

This view removes the imaginary block that seems to stand in the way of sensory, emotional and experiential histories. The mistake is to worry that a particular source plays to conventions, as if *any* source might be free of conventions, as if private thoughts in solitude are free of conventions. Culture is everywhere, even in these moments, and the historian's job is to understand culture in its intersection with human brain–body systems. It is our job to understand the temporal situation and distinct uses of language, of concepts, of the vagaries and vicissitudes of gesture, of signalling, of art and music and letter writing, of drama and fiction and scientific method, of illness and disease and their treatment, of knowledge both lofty and vernacular, of 'common sense' in all its meanings, often alien and often political; and it is our job to put historical testimony of *how it felt* or *what it was like* into these contexts and to take such testimony seriously in its own terms, implicit and explicit source bias included. The history of lived experience is possible. Experience is accessible. It is limited only in the same way that all histories are limited: by scarcity of sources, by partiality, by the limits of empiricism in the archives. But in its essence the experience of the past is no more or less difficult to explain than the experience of the present. Our problem with it actually lies in the deceptive ease with which we understand our own experience, because it appears so plainly to us, *as if* it were natural. Yet we are no less situated than any historical actor. If our own experience seems straightforward both to ourselves and is easy to relay to others, then we simply underestimate what kind of shared concepts, values, signs, etc., it takes to do this. We might try, instead, to imagine explaining our lived experience (let us say, to take a discrete example, of how it feels to try to pay one's gas bill online when the payment website keeps crashing) to a person from the seventeenth century. Where would we begin? This, in reverse, is the historian's challenge in explaining past experience to present readers. Nothing in our shared humanness across time is going to be of much help. But scholarly training certainly will.

The history of experience is certainly possible, even if we concede it is difficult. To pursue it we must finally abandon any notion of a biology beyond culture, of an authenticity under the veneer of convention. To retain these things is to surrender the human, and the meaning of life, to biological essentialism and reductionism.

It will not have escaped the reader that what we propose is a disruption of what it is and means to be human. Here the historicism converges with recent turns in social neuroscience especially and picks up other disciplinary threads to highlight the multiple plasticities that inhere in the human brain–body system. Or, rather, we might call them instabilities. What follows is a brief review of the convergence of these research threads.

4.1 The Permeable Brain–Body

There are any number of pithy statements that might sum up the basic bioconstructionist position of social neuroscientists, but we recount this one, since it is a recent iteration and seems to capture its essence. It is by Hoemann, Devlin and Barrett (2020):

> Advances in neuroscience and computational modeling suggest that the brain operates as an internal model of the body in the world, flexibly recombining previous experience to issue predictions about what sensory input is most likely to occur. These predictions prepare the body for action while simultaneously making meaning of the incoming sensory array. As such, predictions can also be understood as ad hoc concepts that attempt to categorize sensory inputs to achieve a situation-specific purpose. As the developing brain accrues experience, it hones the ability to construct predictions efficiently and according to the concepts of its culture. To categorize sensory inputs as instances of emotion, the developing brain must have previous experiences that have been 'tagged' as these emotions. We hypothesize that emotion words serve this purpose, guiding infants to find functional similarity between instances, and make emotional meaning of their internal and external context ... [T]here are many outstanding questions about emotion concept development, including the exact role words play ... [T]o answer these questions, developmental and affective scientists must work together. We would extend this invitation to linguists, neuroscientists, and more; fully interdisciplinary collaboration is necessary to map the social, physiological, and cognitive mechanisms underlying emotional development ... A predictive processing account of brain function can speak to the highly variable and context-dependent nature of emotion ...

Of particular note, for us, are the concepts of 'world', 'experience' and 'experiences', 'context', 'culture' and 'social mechanisms'. These are regular features of social neuroscientific writing and are central to the ways in which neuroscientists postulate the making of experience. Yet these words tend to be undertheorised and under-scrutinised, being of interest only insofar as they impact what happens in the human interior. It is our view that the position taken up by social neuroscientists puts them humanities-adjacent, and it is historians and anthropologists who can supply a complex account of the 'external' that should enrich neuroscientific accounts of the 'internal'. A biocultural approach can only work if the 'bio' and the 'cultural' are taken equally seriously in the investigation of their dynamic interrelation, without the possibility of separating them back into discrete categories. We note with special interest the call for interdisciplinary collaboration but we mark its limits. Do the humanities fit into the category 'and more' here? In our opinion, and as has been said before, 'We meet ... at the human, having arrived at this phenomenological mystery from opposite disciplinary directions. Unraveling this mystery ought to be a collaborative effort' (Boddice, 2019b, 1996). After all, neither discipline is equipped to go it alone. Encouragingly, we are seeing, especially in neuroscientific research on interoception (Tsakiris and de Preester, 2018), a willingness to engage with the humanities, and there is much to hope for here. Likewise, cultural psychiatrists (Kirmayer and Crafa, 2014; Choudhury and Kirmayer, 2009) have been ideally placed to initiate studies in critical neuroscience in conjunction with cultural studies. The first fruits of this kind of work are forthcoming, but we expect much more (Kirmayer et al, 2020).

Social neuroscientists, then, are fully versed in the language of plasticity, development and cultural dynamics, but their focus is fundamentally and justifiably on the 'internal'. They are interested in what happens inside the brain and body, how things work, how sensations and emotions are produced or, to be more correct, *constructed*. This does raise a question, however, about the contingencies of the cultural dynamics that are essential to neuroplasticity, and it also raises a question about the extent to which the constructions of internal states play a part in cultural contingencies and plasticities. Here we think we might usefully employ a new language of *permeation*, to denote the dynamics of the biocultural brain–body, which both receives 'input' and changes the nature of the 'external' through its 'output'.

The advantage of thinking in terms of permeation is that the dynamic relation between brain–body and world cannot be falsely rendered as directional. Culture does not write to nature; nature does not write to culture. No such separable processes can be entertained in the biocultural view, for they implicitly reify a dualism that we wish to collapse. The brain–body is not *in* the world but *of* the world; the world, in turn, is not made up of brain–bodies, but is embodied. Input and output, if this language is to be entertained, are dynamically connected elements of experiential exchange. The brain–body receives and emits, not as separate processes, but as one continually unstable, contingent process.

How does this play out in the discipline of history? There is already a well-developed historiography of human beings that demonstrates the categorical instability of 'human', and which makes plain the politics of exclusion involved in attempts to render human being as static. Coming to be human has, at various turns, depended on concepts of race, sex, gender, age, species, climate and/or geography and social organisation. It depended on material and social encounter, on the specific contexts of sensory awareness and the associated moral values of both sensation and affect. At times, it relied upon the nature and extent of interaction with other humans, and indeed, animals (Howes, 2018b, vol. 3).[28]

---

[28] Note Massumi, 2018 vol. 3, 279–89; Kitchener, 2018, vol. 3, 363–74.

The brain, as Thomas Fuchs has put it, is but an organ, its processes in constant development but only in a meaningful sense insofar as it is connected and entangled with the body's internal and external systems and the world in which such a body is situated. Humanness, consciousness, conscience, empathy, and so on, are not reducible to the brain, and the brain plays a constituent part in the historical making of these things only to the extent that it is understood as part of a system – brain–body–world – that is characterised by so many contingencies (biological plasticities and cultural change) that its only definitive quality from the point of view of what it means to be human is *instability*.[29] The shifting boundaries of the category 'human' have generally been understood in the humanities to be discursive. Historians and philosophers have focused on the ways in which the construction of the category 'human' has depended on unstable political discourse, in part to challenge our own contemporary lines of exclusion. This has been worthy, but it has depended upon a biological assumption that *actually* the human is and has, in historical time at least, always been the same. The history of the human has, as we have already observed, therefore been limited to discourse analysis, and the old problem of the apparent ease of access to experience, according to the historian's own implicit understanding of their experience as woman, black, subaltern, working class, etc., has undercut the effectiveness of the research into the histories of those excluded from the category 'human' at various historical junctures. We posit here, drawing on and extending the implications of work in the social neurosciences, that there is not only a discursive history of human being, but also an embodied history of being human that understands discourse, or more precisely discursive concepts, to have a material effect. Following Lisa Feldman Barrett's work on the importance of concept development and the bioconstruction of emotion, we suggest that the creation of conceptual categories of what it means to be human, must in turn be formative of what it is like to experience being human. The question then emerges anew about the experience of being denied access to these conceptual categories. In a given context, were those who were excluded aware of the conceptual categories to which they were denied access? Did they have their own, alternative conceptual categories of being? To what extent are the instabilities of these lines of exclusion caused by the accessibility of conceptual categories of being to those who are supposed to be outside?

---

[29] Fuchs (2018, xx) calls the brain an 'organ of mediation', which is 'receptive to lifelong formation through intersubjective and cultural influences: it becomes a social, cultural, and historical organ'. His concluding remark here, that it becomes 'an organ of the human person' must come with the obvious caveat that the 'human person' has been radically disrupted by this account, both conceptually in the present and future, and materially in the past.

Here we are presented with a massive challenge, for those excluded by dominant discourse are often denied the privilege of recording their own, and this occludes their own experience in the historical record. Those experiences emerge at the moments when the lines of exclusion are contested – through feminism, civil rights campaigns, political reform, etc. – and where claims of humanness are registered and weighed. But we must re-examine what it means, at a given juncture, to appeal to a common humanity, for it is often through this appeal that humanity is changed, and we posit that the experience of being human must change with it. This is to say that, from the point of view of how it feels to *be*, there are distinct differences when comparing inside, outside, and on the margins of the category 'human', and that movement from one to the other changes not only a discursive construct but must necessarily alter bioconstructive processes concerning sense and feeling.

It is important at this juncture to remove any room for misinterpretation. It might be objected that we are implying that the lines of exclusion drawn around humanity do in fact indicate the limits of human experience, and that we only get to analyse the experience of 'non-humans' when the lines of exclusion are disrupted by them or for them. Rather, we are following the logical implication that arises from an awareness of conceptual limits. If a set of concepts, including the concept 'human', defines what it is, what it means, and how it feels to be human, and if those concepts are not available to those for whom such concepts are explicitly denied, then to examine the experience of these excluded others through those very concepts is either simply erroneous or, worse, an implicit endorsement of those exclusionary concepts and the politics that underwrites them. In order to access the experience of the excluded we need access to *their* conceptual map, to their perception of reality. And precisely here, we run into the limits of historical research. To riff here on the work of Kennetta Hammond Perry, when lived experience is represented archivally only by the documentation of violation or exclusion, then the recovery of lived experience is actually an illusion.[30] We cannot shine a light on these lives, but only on the power that diminished them. We must admit that this is a terminal limit of the history of experience, but it prompts other, no less important work, concerning the ways in which power is held, justified and used precisely to impose such a limit, in order deliberately to overwrite or silence experience. Where we, as historians of experience, run into this wall is precisely the moment at which we become

---

[30] Based on her work on the life of David Oluwale and the Alchemy of Policing Blackness in Britain, keynote address at the Northeast Conference on British Studies, Montreal, October 2019.

able to see or reveal the extent of the power to erase, whether this power is held by a state, or by some other form of authority.

This does not mean the history of experience is impossible, however, though it does tend to hone our attention on the moments at which others become visible or hearable in the archive, at those moments at which they claim a stake in the category 'human' and thereby change that category. The question, 'Am I not a man and a brother?' plays upon what is held in common, but its political intent shifts the discursive register of the category 'man', and with it the range of concepts and experiences associated with shared belonging within that category. Likewise, the question 'Are women human?', as recovered from the archive by Joanna Bourke, does not operate on the notion that 'human' is a fixed category, from which female membership has been overlooked, but on the notion that 'human' is a political category, maintained for the advantage of a select group (white men), at the expense of others disallowed any humanity (women, non-white men). Other historians (Hartman, 1997; 2007) have employed a notion of 'composite portraiture' – a rhetorical device rather than a photographic one – that allows for the probabilistic rendering, the 'critical fabulation' of experience based on the aggregation of many different sources and a preponderance of silence. Even then, such an approach might emphasise the mechanisms by which humanity, subjectivity and meaningful experience are denied. And it makes historical writing self-consciously creative, even fictive, placing difficult demands on the historian to justify claims of truth. But, for certain topics, one can be more confident at least of the successful reconstruction of context. For oral historians, the possibilities of using this approach look fruitful, where the testimony they collect is either extremely dense, covering many hundreds or even thousands of sources, or rather thin on the ground, comprised of fragments.[31]

4.2 History, Brain and Body (Politic)

Famously, Aristotle (1944, 1253a) declared us political animals, a product of membership of social communities with the ability to apply reason, speech and social instinct when navigating the shoals of communal knots. If he was right, is it possible to discern the reasons why we, as political animals, hold the ideological beliefs we hold? Why do we embrace certain political opinions and reject others? Some answers to these almost audacious questions we already

---

[31] See the work of Heidi Morrison, *Surviving Memory in Palestine: Narrative, Trauma, and Children of the Second Intifada* (in production), drawing in turn on the work of Lawrence-Lightfoot and Hoffman Davis, 1997 and on Hunt, 2012, which highlights the social and cultural factors that shape and re-shape subjective experience. Thanks to Heidi Morrison for alerting us to these possibilities.

know. Class, income, age, education, all influence how we vote and why. But there is rather more to it than that. Here, we unpack how history, the natural and social sciences, emotion and the sensory are all needed and mutually essential for accessing what it means to experience in the past.

The study of what has been called, in rather too cavalier a fashion, 'disgustology' explores the ways in which emotion, psychology, biology and the senses influence our political leanings. At base, the field is a product of ostensibly disparate scholars asking constructive questions of one another. Political scientists in particular have recruited the expertise of neuroscientists and social psychologists to divine why we vote as we do (and by 'we' they mean, on the whole, citizens in western democracies). The upshot of their findings is simple but startling: they claim, persuasively, that modern political behaviour – across a variety of modern democracies – is in part biologically inherited and revealed in our physiological reaction to perceived threats. There are, an emerging body of research shows, definite neural responses to images, tastes and scents commonly deemed emotionally 'disgusting' in the context of what is commonly understood as 'modern' society. Conservatives and liberals both react to, for example, disgusting images, especially images of contamination, filthy toilets, mutilation, sores and the like. But they do so in different ways, with some 95 per cent of reactions being predictable and reproducible.[32]

The emotion of 'disgust' is central to these political beliefs. Violent images (guns, accidents, gore) or beautiful, pleasing images (smiling children, sumptuous landscapes, laughter) do not have the same predictive power as disgusting images. Many studies have revealed that people with a more conservative ethos (holding beliefs in, for example, the desirability of social hierarchy and authority, sexual conservatism and a distrust of outsiders or others) demonstrate a higher sensitivity to images conventionally deemed disgusting. Political scientist, Michael Bang Petersen of Denmark's Aarhus University, maintains that 'disgust influences our political views as much as or even more than long-recognized factors such as education and income bracket' (Petersen quoted in McAuliffe, 2019).

If the association between political opinion and disgust is apparent, what is less certain is why. At first blush, it seems odd that images of, say, vomit should inspire (or associate with) one's views on immigration or religion. Plainly, there is nothing inherently political about the emotion of disgust. Disgust occurs outside of political contexts all the time and politics can, plainly, exist

---

[32] Exemplary popular summaries of the issue include McAuliffe, 2019 (our discussion relies on this fine article). A more scholarly synopsis with its own specific argument is Ahn et al, 2014. Other relevant work includes Jost, Federico and Napier, 2009; Alford, Funk and Hibbing, 2005. More generally, see Clarke, Hoggett and Thompson, 2006, and Neuman, 2007.

independently of ideas about disgust. But if we think of disgust as serving as a warning, a way to protect us from infection, the emotion–political equation begins to make better sense. We search, often unwittingly, using all our senses, for signs of infection in the world: mould, sores, garbage, stench, fetor, bitterness, and the like. We tend to withdraw from these sensory impressions because we interpret them as disgusting and dangerous; a sort of behavioural immune system is at work. Work by social psychologists suggests that this type of germ radar operates on a default system of better-safe-than-sorry and is especially prone to reading other human beings in this light. Being germ-aware can affect how we react to and perceive people of a different background, race, or ethnicity. There is something of a history to this: psychologists and biologists have theorised that in the past foreigners would have been most likely to expose native populations to germs and pathogens and that this exposure has evolved into a modern-day xenophobia. More finely grained analyses support this theory. In the United States, recent work shows that resistance to immigration is most pronounced in those states with the highest incidence of (and worry about) infectious diseases, thereby reaffirming other work which establishes a close association between a high disgust sensitivity and nervousness about strangers, not just foreigners, in general. For this reason, social psychologists can predict, across a wide range of polities, how people will vote. Perhaps the best-known example was the 2008 US Presidential election between John McCain and Barack Obama. States exhibiting the greatest fear of germs not only reported that they were more likely to vote for the Republican candidate (McCain) but, in fact, did so (McAuliffe, 2019; Inbar et al., 2012).

While much of this research takes visual images as their disgust-cue or trigger, some studies deploy olfaction and smell and with equally arresting results. Smell is sufficiently potent to shape reaction, even within a group of people who share similar political ideologies. One such experiment split a politically uniform sample of people into two groups. One was subjected to a vomit-like smell; the other was placed in a relatively deodorised setting. Both groups completed a survey identifying their social values. The group exposed to the smell of vomit consistently recorded greater opposition to things such as gay rights, premarital sex, pornography, and topics deemed blasphemous or loosely disgusting. Other putrid smells elicit similar responses. Journalist Kathleen McAuliffe puts it this way: 'When we experience disgust, we tend to make harsher moral judgments'. In this instance, bad smells might well serve as an especially powerful disgust trigger not least because neurologically and physiologically smell is thoroughly transgressive, invasive, has an immediate impact (courtesy of the absence of nose-lids), and is indexed to long-term memory. To breathe is to live and the transgressive nature of smell might well reaffirm deep-seated fears of disease and provide little to no filter to stop the behavioural immune system from kicking in.

Disgustology does important work. It applies emotion theory to a real world issue and insistent problem (politics) by actively engaging the sensate in an effort to account for human experience. Moreover, it demonstrates that a full understanding of why people vote the way they do cannot be reliably expressed without reference to emotion and the senses. More prosaically, it grants researchers access to the ability to emphasise the 'relevance' and 'impact' of their work, both important metrics for securing scholarly funding in western societies.

What role, if any, does history play in all of this?

What little historical work that has been done on the specific problem of relating disgust to political opinion is suggestive. McAuliffe rightly and helpfully reminds us of the etymology of the word 'disgust'. In English, its derivation is from Middle French, *desgoust*, literally 'distaste'. This might seem like a merely interesting footnote until we realise that taste, too, serves as a predictor of political opinion. Conservatives, it turns out, are better at detecting bitter – and, therefore, more disgusting – compounds in foods than are liberals. Part of this is genetically determined, with the number of taste receptors on people's tongues varying widely. Researchers have found that people who are more conservative tend to have a denser concentration of fungiform papillae making their taste more acute. This perhaps explains why a 2009 survey of over 60,000 Americans found a split between the taste preferences of liberals and conservatives. The former favoured bitter-tasting arugula twice as often as did conservatives (McAuliffe, 2019).[33]

Still, whatever the sense (sight, smell, taste) and its relationship to feelings of disgust, important problems remain, ones best revealed – and resolved – through the lens of history. What, for example, do we make of political voting patterns apparent prior to the discovery of germ theory in the 1890s? Can we make anything meaningful of them? If disgustology is to make consistent ontological sense, it cannot tether itself to breezy claims about the transcendence of the emotion of disgust or the universal sense of what smells disgusting or malodorous and how that might or might not impact political choices. As it stands, that is precisely what disgustology does: it implicitly claims a universal truth precisely because it does not take seriously historical context. Historical context has the potential to undermine or reaffirm the main claims of disgustology; either way, historical context needs to be taken seriously if disgustology is to have legs.

---

[33] See also the foundational work by Kolnai, 2004 and the insightful collection, Delville, Norris and Von Hoffmann, 2015. Both works make the case that any full understanding of the emotion of disgust must be accessed through interdisciplinary study and be in sustained dialogue with work on perception and the senses.

Some recent work highlights the importance of placing the very emotion of (and senses associated with) disgust into appropriate historical context. Bettina Hitzer's (2020a) work on the association between the emotion of disgust, smell and moral assessment among twentieth-century German cancer patients and medical professionals shows with unusual precision how emotion and the senses evolved over time. In the nineteenth century, changes in medical knowledge and treatment altered not the smell of cancer but the ways in which doctors smelled the disease. Cancer, prior to the mid-nineteenth century, was something to be managed in palliative fashion; advances in medicine led doctors to try to cure the disease, which altered the ways in which doctors smelled tumours. Smell became less reliable as a diagnostic tool and operations to attempt to remove cancer brought doctors into more direct contact with the smell of tumours. The association between disgust and the scent of tumours became more pronounced, with the smell of cancerous humans now framed in terms of animal excrement.

Other developments were important for reconfiguring how people judged the meaning of smells and, by association, what they understood as disgusting. Courtesy of the work of Robert Koch and Louis Pasteur and the emergence of germ theory in the 1890s, the idea that smells could transmit diseases (the miasma theory) lost a great deal of currency. Still, both miasma theory and germ theory had the effect of shaping urban smellscapes especially since both, at some level, connected bad smells with diseases and germs. Sanitation efforts shuttled stench underground, required better ventilation in houses, and mandated the use of piped fresh water. These material changes, in turn, altered the way people understood what they smelled. With wretched smells (relatively) diluted, from urban areas mainly, people became increasingly sensitive to the smells that remained or that popped up courtesy of further urban development. Because people continued to associate smell with disease generally the very idea of healthfulness and proper bourgeois morals became indexed to the idea of deodorisation and the absence of smells. This larger trend, says Hitzer (2020a), was reflected in twentieth-century German hospitals where the absence of smell was preferred, the smell of antiseptic accepted (which became almost definitive of the ideal hospital smellscape), and bad smells designated as hazardous not because they were agents of contamination but because they were associated with substances believed to be infectious, such as excrement.[34]

In the 1920s and 1930s, German physicians treating cancer expanded the meaning of the smell of the disease and, in the process, recalibrated the emotional meaning of disgust. They increasingly described the smell of cancerous patients as disgusting to not only their noses but to that of other patients and

---

[34] See also Corbin, 1986; Kiechle, 2017; Jütte, 2019.

visiting family members. One solution was to segregate cancer patients and contain the disgust they inspired from non-terminal patients. Embedded here was the idea that cancer patients themselves could not experience or detect the sort of disgust their stench inspired in others. All of this, of course, was occurring in the context of publicly articulated ideas associating race with smell and disgust more generally. The stench of the tumour became political in this context; the putative stench of Medieval Jews was resurrected; Jews were now associated with stinking cancerous tumours, disgusting leeches on the body politic of the Third Reich (Hitzer, 2020).[35]

Hitzer finds that after 1945 and the demise of the Third Reich, the vocabulary connecting smell and disgust and cancer evaporated. Not only was cancer itself increasingly dissociated from smell in the 1950s but the connection between smell and disgust was severed. Hitzer argues that this dissociation was not due to any real changes in the treatment of cancer (treatments which may have lessened the stench of tumours, for example) but, rather, is explicable in terms of a shift in the meanings of disgust. Nurses, for example, were urged in medical manuals to overcome this emotion when dealing with cancer patients, to tamp it down, and mask their reaction. The feeling of disgust was now *verboten*, an emotion to be quarantined. Hitzer maintains that this dissociation was multi-causal. The demise of the Third Reich effectively disentangled smell and disgust and destabilised any moral legitimacy connecting the two. Guilt too was at work here, a reaction to the recent and appalling appetite for racial and ethnic persecution. In effect, the association between smell and disgust both socially and medically had been broken after World War II. Disgust was situational and historical context provides important clues enabling us to see how and why its meaning changed. Any long-term study of disgustology needs to keep in mind the idea that context matters a great deal.

Not all diseases can reliably index disgust and political persuasion. Very recent history is powerfully instructive in reminding us that other emotions can function in a way that inverts political models of disgustology. Even as we write, the world struggles with the Coronavirus pandemic and beyond the talk of curve flattening, quarantining, and silent spreading is a shift in emotions and political sensibilities accompanied by a different set of sensory triggers. Disgustology no longer fully explains political leanings and behaviour. If it did, then, in the US at least, people of liberal political persuasion would be less disgusted at the prospect of the virus; germ/virus-fearing conservatives would be more disgusted and call for a tightening of measures to contain the source of their disgust. Available data, although naturally still preliminary, suggests something

---

[35] See also Smith, 2012.

else is at work. Democrats and liberals, whether they live in urban, suburban or rural environments, are the ones calling for much greater protection; conservatives are not. A Pew Research Center survey recently showed that 80 per cent of Democrats supported closing non-essential businesses; the figure among Republicans: 60 per cent. The reason for this might well be that COVID-19 has introduced a different emotion and a different sensory register, one quite distinct from disgust. That emotion is not disgust but fear. Available surveys ask the extent to which people are 'scared' of the virus. The political alignments show that liberals are more fearful of it than are conservatives (Zitner, McCormick and Chinni 2020). Because the virus is invisible, because it tends to deaden the senses of smell and taste, new sensory metrics are at work. (Rabin, 2020). Our point here is that emotions are not politically stable in light of disease and it is the specificity of context that allows us to see and detect shifts. A virus that fools the eyes, induces anosmia, and deadens taste has, it seems, the ability to invite emotional shifts at a very fundamental level of political persuasion but it can only be understood historically by attending to context.[36]

History is instructive in other ways. Let's take a political circumstance not dissimilar to the current context that has allowed disgustology to make some persuasive claims about political ideology and voting behaviours, a period equally fraught, equally partisan, equally veined with emotion: the couple of decades leading up to the US Civil War, still the bloodiest conflict in US history. There are other historical examples, of course, detailing how emotions mobilised political sentiment in post–World War II Germany (Bessel, 2005) and the French Revolution (Reddy, 2000), but this instance works in helpful parallel to work done on disgustology, most of which is US in nature (Torre, 2007; Eustace, 2008).[37]

The eruption of the US Civil War in 1861 was prefaced by remarkably heightened and demonstrably emotional partisan political discourse beginning at least in the 1830s and roiling into fever pitch especially in the 1840s and 1850s. The division was, simply put, between a slaveholding South, heavily vested in the economic benefit and cultural meaning of enslavement, and a growing abolitionist and free labour sentiment in the Northern states. The atmospherics were as tense then as they are now, and emotions ran high.

But which emotions mattered and why? At some level, the visual images associated with disgust in the US in the 2000s were at play in the decades leading up to the US Civil War, especially in the 1840s and 1850s. Abolitionists and anti-slavery activists in the North seized upon (and produced) drawings and

---

[36] For the breakdown of political beliefs and fear, see Zitner, McCormick and Chinni, 2020; on the impact of the virus on the senses of smell, see Rabin, 2020.

[37] See also Matich, 2009; Kuntsman, 2009.

visual representations as evidence of the moral enormity of human bondage and degeneracy of southern slaveholders. Posters, newspapers, novels, poetry, all contained written and visual depictions of the savagery of southern bondage; many depicted, quite vividly, the physical and emotional cruelty of the South's 'peculiar institution'. These images were mobilised to animate anti-slavery support and bolster the formation of a party dedicated to freedom: the Republican Party, founded in 1854. The vividness of the drawings, etchings and narratives were highly emotional in tone and by design.

Sight was not the only sense in use here. Auditory triggers, actual and metaphorical, also played their part. Novels and tracts offered gruesome descriptions of the sounds of slaves screaming, the crack of the whip, the crushing silence of voices in a slaveholding south and compared these soundscapes to those of the (imagined) North: the hum of industry, the sound of democracy and the tenor of free men labouring. More tangibly, anti-slavery activists attempted to recreate the sounds of bondage. Sometimes, abolitionists dropped chains on stage in front of northern abolitionist audiences to let them hear the signature sound of bondage. It was an auditory device used to cast southern slaveholders as uniquely un-American, prone to bouts of extraordinary violence; emotionally numbed individuals who were unable to feel the pain of others (Smith, 2001).

But what, precisely, were the emotions being used and deployed in this context? We know what they were not. One emotion that was not permitted full expression in the context of antebellum political culture was anger. As Michael Woods (2011, 692) has argued:

> Throughout the generation preceding the Civil War, Americans waged a 'steady war' against anger in domestic life because they believed that the emotion threatened the relationships idealized by the cult of domesticity. This aversion to anger extended into politics, particularly among those who conceived of the nation as a family writ large. In a country knit together by 'mutual harmony and good feeling among all its members', emotions which destroyed those harmonious feelings, as anger was liable to do, were politically unacceptable.

Anger blinded reason, thought contemporaries, and the emotion existed uncomfortably within the moral and ethical coordinates of mid-nineteenth-century America.[38]

All of this was thoroughly politicised and designed to animate what we might think of as a political base today. But the operative emotional discourse was not one of disgust. Disgust was, of course, woven into political discourse. Some southerners, for example, expressed disgust with the very idea of the Union. But

---

[38] More generally, see Woods, 2014.

at work here was an emotion that was far more germane then than it is now: indignation. While indignation occasionally bisected with feelings of disgust and anger, these were more components of indignation than standalone, politically situated emotions. In fact, few references to being disgusted, North or South, circulated in political discourse at the time. The reasons for the pronounced appeal to indignation in the years leading up to the Civil War are several. First, indignation had a history in American political discourse, originating in the colonial period. Second, because it was not raw anger, indignation was deemed respectable and appropriate as a means to express frustration with political opponents. Most importantly, indignation was acceptable because it gave fuller expression to another prevailing and long-term emotion, that of sympathy; sympathy for the oppressed, a humanitarian impulse common to much of the Atlantic world at the time. Indignation was understood as 'sympathetic anger', a form of compassionate outrage, a spin on righteous anger mixed with compassion. In fact, indignation was almost a moral requisite for Americans. As one commented in 1846: 'Without indignation against cruelty, fraud, falsehood, disorder, the virtues would not have their full force in the mind'. As Woods (2011, 693) rightly remarks: 'Those deficient in indignation lacked a moral compass and could not recognize justice'. The immediate reasons behind the uptick in indignation in this period – one marked by increasing numbers of indignation meetings, mostly in the North but not unknown in the South – need not concern us here and are well documented by Woods. Suffice to say, indignation leading up to the Civil War was a rough equivalent to the role played by disgust in today's political discourse.[39]

Indignation in the 1840s and 1850s seems to have done the work that disgust does in the modern era. At base, it served as a form of emotional valorisation: Northerners used indignation to claim emotional superiority in their embrace of – and ability to feel – certain emotions. Slaveholders were either violent brutes or emotionally numb, unable to feel or understand the growing transatlantic humanitarian sentiment, unable to imagine the emotional and physical pain of others. Emotion in politics, in this context, then, served to politicise emotion itself and, in turn, functioned as a broad and admittedly clumsy proxy for political sentiment: those able to feel the pain of others tended towards the ideology of the free soil, free labour, anti-slavery platform of the newly formed Republican party; those who did not were slaveholding southerners wedded to any party but the Republican party (which drew its support exclusively from Northern states) and inclined to support old-style Democrats (a party which operated in both sections of the country). Northern indignation at (and claims

---

[39] On sympathy and humanitarianism, see Clark, 1995; Halttunen, 1995; and Haskell, 1985.

of) Southern emotional cruelty and intransigence was an historically and con-textually mediated form of disgust, casting slaveholders as increasingly irre-deemable others, a people to be rightly excluded from the American body politic. For their part, Southern slaveholders embraced indignation to portray Northern abolitionists as intractable outsiders, sores on the Republic, and agents of disruption. Sight and sound functioned in ways eerily like the way the senses accent the political economy of disgust today and with a similar result: a heightened polarisation and emotional form of partisanship.

We do not, of course, have access to sophisticated polling data from the nineteenth century; nor are we able to subject antebellum Americans to the same sort of detailed social psychological testing conducted today. Still, what appears clear from Michael Wood's work on indignation and Bettina Hitzer's work on cancer and disgust is that we do not need to view the broad question of political ideology and emotion as transcendent; instead, history allows us to refine the connection, situating the general association of ideology and political sensibil-ity and emotion into specific contexts. Those contexts tell us that emotion generally and political persuasion are indexed; that the senses play an important role in informing the emotion at play; and that the emotion that informs political persuasion changes over time according to historical context and according to the situated boundaries of being human. The point we wish to stress here is that history allows us to reap the rewards of the natural sciences without surrender-ing to the universalist conceit embedded in some of its claims: where at the level of lived experience the emotions, senses and cognition are interrelated and entangled, it is not profitable to disassociate them. Such a disassociation is itself an historical specificity that has reality-producing effects in its own time, but to project it onto other times where it does not belong only serves to desiccate our understanding of past experience.

5 Dynamics

Recasting the human as a worlded body–mind system, suggests a new way of understanding historical causality as it pertains to human behaviour and affective practices. With the collapse of various dyads – nature/culture, body/mind, con-scious/unconscious, intentional/unintentional, expression/feeling – the binary of cause/effect also dissolves into dynamic biocultural processes in which humans take part. Experience is shaped relationally. To make this case, we offer a critical assessment and enfolding of the various neurohistorical projects into our new history of experience. Since this work emphasises brain–body historicity, bodily practices, psychotropic stimuli, microevolution and epigenetics, it offers a ripe opportunity to frame research on affective/sensitive experience of humans as individual and social biocultural beings, to think in terms of 'contexts of possibility' and the limits of biocultural experience. We suggest that this can take us, as Lynn Hunt (2009) forecast, to an understanding of 'how it felt to be there, then', but also further than this, to the relationship between experience and 'events'. Making claims about what humanity is, even making such claims on biological grounds, necessarily affects the meaning of humanity, and with it the possibility for experience also changes. A tight focus on these moments must do something also to our notion of causality and of the 'event'. We exemplify all of this while engaging critically with questions of relationality and the experience of exclusion through animal studies and post-humanism (or thinking eco-historically).

How does an historically excluded individual or an excluded group, those classified as non-human – women, slaves, racial others – emerge and lay claim to inclusion? How does the experiential realm of feeling human become available and gain recognition, when before it was out of bounds? There are, of course, social, cultural, economic and institutional, as well as individual precipitating factors. These are the traditional grounds of historical causation and we shall not abandon them. We will, however, augment them. Reincorporating the brain–body into historical analysis as an historical artefact means we must also account for the changes in the brain–body and the changes it brings about. Since we have characterised the brain–body as existing in dynamic relation with the world in which it is situated, we must in turn understand the brain–body as something that does not merely show the effects of cultural change, but which also has a causative quality. With the collapse of the nature–culture dyad into an understanding of the human as biocultural, we are left with a continuous process of inscription and re-inscription, of a dynamic process of cause and effect between brain–body and world (Boddice, 2018b).

How to make sense of this in practical, historical terms? Conceptual history, indebted fundamentally to Reinhart Koselleck (2002), provides a clue and, given the importance that concepts have assumed in the understanding of brain development and the construction of experience (Gendron et al., 2012; Hoemann, Xu and Barrett, 2019), it should be pursued, though we must treat with great caution Koselleck's need for an 'anthropological constant' (2002, 45–75). While a given concept has an orthodox interpretation and reception, it is also subject to other interpretations. Concepts can be lived out, as it were, plurally. The success of an emotional regime, in Reddy's (2001) terms, may depend on the extent to which a set of emotion concepts are secured against alternative 'readings', through which the same emotion concepts might provide emotive success to an outside group. Put another way, excluded groups often share a physical space and a language with the group that excludes them, and this gives them access to the concepts against which they are formally defined.

If those concepts are appropriated, re-worked, literally re-constructed in the brain, then a potential biocultural factor of resistance emerges out of the very concepts that define the orthodoxy. The master concepts (for example, 'human', 'civilised', 'rational', 'emotional', 'sensitive') are also in process of revision and augmentation, through other languages and other cultural experiences, existing within or adjacent to the orthodoxy. Human exchange, however asymmetrical the power relations, has the effect of mixing and disrupting master concepts, which renders cultural orthodoxies unstable and changes brain development, alters brain predictions, makes emotional and sensory experience anew. The human – this biocultural dynamic being – is always unstable. The plasticity of its brain–body system makes it primed to 'see' things in new ways, just as cultural fluidity tends to present it with new situations.

Social neuroscience has concerned itself with the importance of concepts and language, but there has also been significant attention paid to the vicissitudes of facial expression. It seems as if the universalist view, that human facial expressions are essentially the same everywhere and can be used to tap automatic and universal emotions, is finally shattered beyond repair (Leys, 2017; Barrett et al., 2019, Reddy, 2020). It is, we think, important to extend our own historical analysis of concepts and human development to include non-verbal 'concepts' such as gesture, expression (facial and whole body) (Boddice, 2019d; Pernau and Rajamani, 2016; Rajamani, 2016), non-verbal sounds, modes of touch, valuations of smell and sight, and matters of taste (aesthetic and physical),[40] as well as various other senses including 'common' sense (Boddice, 2019c, 112–15), pain (Boddice, 2014; Bourke, 2014; Moscoso, 2012), stress, and the sense of self, one factor in which is interoception (Tsakiris and de Preester, 2018). All of these things are experienced through constructive processes in the brain–body that are embedded in socio-cultural-temporal settings that make them meaningful (or that make them meaningless, to the non-initiate; see Moscoso, 2016). They are intersected with and dynamically related to micro-evolutionary and epigenetic processes, the scientific understanding of which is in its infancy. All of this is part of what being human means, and all of it is instrumental in the delimitation of the category 'human'. It is all part of the biocultural dynamic that makes the human unstable. This, in turn, explains human change (and is thereby a factor in historical causation). Asking about these things alters our engagement with the archive, for such questions presuppose these phenomena to be historical where they were previously assumed to

---

[40] In addition to the kinds of sensory history frequently referenced here, Susan Lanzoni's (2018) history of empathy is useful, especially in its early chapters that show just how mutable matters of aesthetic sensibility and their valuation have been.

be universal, if they were considered at all. They are all fair game in the rebuilding of 'contexts of possibility'.

We cannot lay any claim to the coining of the phrase 'contexts of possibility', but we can extend its utility. The phrase was coined, in passing, in the doctoral thesis of Fanny H. Brotons (2017) (riffing, in turn, on Koselleck's (2002) 'conditions of possibility of experience'), which concerned the experience of cancer in Spain in the nineteenth century. 'Even in the cases in which our sick ancestors did not produce any personal record of what they lived through, it is still possible to reconstruct ... the context of possibilities in which the understanding of the illness they went through was grounded' (20). The truth of this sentence seems immediately obvious upon reading it. It is so simple, so straightforward. Yet it is entirely innovative and groundbreaking. Its power as an analytical perspective lies in the removal of 'objective' understandings of disease and pain. As medical knowledge of cancer has improved, this knowledge has worked its way into historical analysis, such that the historian can seemingly weave two distinct narratives: what the patient said, on the one hand, and what was *really* happening, on the other. Thinking in terms of the context of possibilities removes the risk of this kind of reading, instead collapsing what the patient said into a context of what the patient could have known, at the time, about the disease and its symptoms and course. This is weighed alongside the modes of expression available to the patient, and the encounters of the patient with medical personnel, authority, medicine, and social and interpersonal modes of care, to make sense of the *situated* reality of the disease as it was experienced at the time. Even where the patient leaves no record of the experience of the disease, the context of possibilities for this experience is much more readily recovered, and reveals the historicity of suffering, salving and the experience of dying. What cancer *is* becomes secondary, to the historian, to how cancer *feels*, both for the person with the disease and for those who encounter them (see also Moscoso and Zaragoza, 2014). Moreover we assert that the experience of cancer becomes intrinsic to what cancer *is*, because the social reception and vernacular knowledge of the disease is central to the way it is researched and treated, encountered and valued (Hitzer, 2020b). Whatever cancer *is* on a cellular level has no 1:1 bearing on what it is like to have it.

5.1 Events and Agency

To take the human out of biological stasis must, in turn, change what we mean by the word 'event', for it becomes difficult, if not impossible, and perhaps undesirable to isolate events from the biocultural dynamic. Experience is fluid. Discrete things in the world that 'happen' are experienced as such by the brain through a constructive process that includes the prior experience of the individual and the social relations (including potentially different kinds of perceptions of the self), and the cultural conceptual web in which the individual is caught. An event, insofar as we care about events only as they are interpreted and lived by people, therefore, is always part of the process of human being, part of the biocultural dynamic (see also our comments on memory, Section 3.1). We might, we suspect, be accused of robbing the individual of agency. We respond in two ways, first by gesturing at the instability of the individual as self, second by exposing the risks of maintaining the rhetoric of agency as it tends to be deployed and by ultimately rejecting the concept's usefulness.

We have already dealt, in passing, with the plural ways in which humans have perceived of the self, as socially constituted and as individually constituted. To this we might add those cases where the self-reference to the first person is not available. If the 'I' is denied to a being then it is not certain by any means that such a being could still think of itself in terms of selfhood, or of having any individual agency. The concept 'I' has to be acquired. If it is not, then what is the experience of the being with no 'I'? We can, of course, assign such a being's humanity in taxonomic terms, and doing so obviously serves a political interest, but a true history of experience has to take seriously the experience of those who have been cast without the category human. To mark the ways in which the politics of exclusion are inscribed on the interior, influencing and delimiting the ways in which situated biology is *permitted* to engage, dynamically, with the exterior, is imperative if we are to understand what discourse does to bodies (and vice versa).[41]

Agency, it seems to us, often comes bundled with 'authenticity' (see Section 4), and refers to an element of individual autonomy, a course of human action that is parcelled off from the biocultural dynamic and available to the individual as a course of independent conscious cognitive consideration and action. Where is the evidence for this? Agency is a political concept.[42] To be encultured in an environment in which this concept is available doubtless fosters the experience

---

[41] See, in particular, Meloni, 2019 and Stenner, 2017. Stenner is particularly wary of the turn to affect where affect is isolated 'from other modes of experience as if it were a pristine state of unqualified autonomy' – this is the basis of 'affect theory', and a prime reason for throwing it out – and warns that we must 'rethink affect as referring to a range of liminal phenomena tightly connected to vectors of transition, always in concrete historical settings involving multi-layered flows of embodied interaction' (203). The phrase 'situated biology', and its parent idea 'local biology', belong to Lock (1993) first, and are given further scientific and political traction in Lock, 2017. For an example of its use, see Brotherton and Nguyen, 2013a and 2013b.

[42] The conceptual work of Vallgårda, Alexander and Olsen, 2015, 2018, for example, seeks to 'dismantle the notion of the rational, fundamentally free and autonomous individual and to find better ways of analysing the historically contingent emotions, interactions, and confrontations of the past'.

of its action and must, also, be causative of political and discursive change. We should not, however, be fooled into thinking that 'agency' has an objective existence outside of human situated biology, any more than there are deep-seated underlying emotions that are truly 'authentic' in a pure, universal and timeless way. Discussions about agency tend to polarise. The denial of agency leads to an assumption either that human action is entirely biologically determined or else inflexibly culturally prescribed. We say it is neither. To talk of 'programming', whether by nature or by nurture, is reductive and unhelpful. Biocultural dynamics permit, more or less, a range of experiences, choices, expressions, and so on. The extent to which this range is available depends upon the specific time, place, culture, structures of power, concepts, and so on. Indeed, there must always be *some* range of experience and action, or else there would be no possibility of change. The dynamic of culture and biology, as we have said, is implicitly unstable. The human is not in stasis – not bound either by biology or by culture – and therefore causes change through its range of practices and experiences, within the context of possibility in a given time and place. Insofar as this range exists, it might be possible to refer to emotive processes as a form of agency, but we suspect that retaining this label would be misleading and misunderstood by most. 'Agency', therefore, should still have a place within historiographical practice as an object of research in those contexts where the concept of agency was available to the historical actors themselves. As an end of research, that is, the process of doing historical research in order to reveal the 'agency' of historical actors anywhere and at any time, it should be cast aside. Putting agency where it does not strictly belong is no more valid than the projection of universal emotions to all people in all places and times, or the claim that human beings are fundamentally biologically universal across historical time.

5.2 Politics

What are the implications of re-intensifying historiographical focus on the human in this way, when the humanities are already in the throes of post-humanism, and where history itself has been challenged to think relationally, ecologically, beyond the traditional limits set by archival empiricism? Our conjecture is that such a focus, constructed in this way, actually permits new critical possibilities in precisely these directions. To take the human out of its biological stasis while also grounding discursive social constructivism in the body necessarily raises the question of context, relationality, materiality, encounter and interaction. The need to know what factors come to make the situated human becomes urgent. Situated worlds are essential to the history of experience. As per Dominic LaCapra's (2009) agenda, to think of the human as unstable, made according to contingencies of context and contexts of possibility, not only does away with implicit biological essentialism for humans, but also for other beings too. If we take seriously the argument that those excluded from the category 'human' had distinct historical experiences according to their access to conceptual awareness of themselves and their society, then we also have to take seriously the lack of stability in the categories 'animal' and 'nature'. Both categories are conceptual linguistic constructions that have their own histories, neither of which contains or refers to anything intrinsic to the beings or matter that they aim to define. Insofar as such categories are entwined with human conceptual constructions of self, society and world, they are vital parts of the context in which humans are made and changed, and in which humans experience themselves as such. This has the effect of de-politicising historiography in certain crucial ways, and of re-politicising it in new ways.

First, the language and politics of rights become limited to historical analyses of times and places where 'rights' were available to historical actors, and should be understood in historical terms. Similarly, political and social activism connected to gender, sexuality, race, mental health, and so on, must be understood in historical context and must not be projected to times and places where these categories were not in play. Any attempt to impose, after the fact, an identity, a diagnosis, a way of thinking even, that was not possibly available to the historical actor in question, only undermines the political intent of the historian. It essentialises precisely where it should deconstruct. It refers, in Scott's terms, to something 'foundational', precisely when it should historicise reflexively. We must remove the timeless ethical/political stance that is sometimes explicit but more often implicit in historical works that cross over into political activism. While not denying the importance of such work, from a strictly historiograph-ical point of view contemporary politics are almost always unfit for making historical arguments because they fall into anachronism at the first move. From the point of view of the history of the senses, the history of emotions, and the history of experience, this kind of approach immediately risks misrepresenting how historical actors felt. But we might reverse this equation and think instead of the utility of historical arguments for *making* contemporary politics, as will be discussed in the following.

Second, we have to acknowledge a frontier that is difficult to overcome. It is already difficult enough to try and reconstruct the sensory and affective worlds of those excluded from the category human, whose experiences only really emerge for us as historians when they demand a change to that category so as to be permitted membership of it. What, then, of non-humans who can never make such claims? Social neuroscientists who have emphasised the importance of concepts in emotional development and experience have pointed out the unavoidable chasm this creates in exploring or understanding the emotions or experiences of those beings whose concepts remain utterly alien to us because there is no access to language or other signification *in their own terms*. There have been some casual but not credible claims that this type of neuroscience risks a kind of neo-Cartesianism, or a grand denial that animals feel anything at all. Such a risk should be dispelled: 'Only a fool would argue that animals don't have an affective life. But the gap between humans who use linguistic conceptual constructions that we can access and understand, and animals that do not, represents a serious ontological and epistemological problem' (Boddice, 2019a, 99).[43] To infer from human concepts, which become all the more varied and situated when seen through the historical lens, the emotional or experiential life of non-humans is to engage in a fallacy of logical inference.[44] It is straightforward to say that animals have affective experiences, but far from straightforward to say that these experiences can be understood through a modern conceptual framework in the English language. We can project and speculate, but such projections and speculations will say something more about us than about the experience of the animals. Here is a limitation, but also an opportunity. When we look at the history of such fallacious thinking, we gain an important insight into the ways in which situated human experiences were formed, expressed and reinforced by incorporation within scientific orthodoxies.[45] That such thinking is still not only popular, but indeed at the centre of ethology and evolutionary biology should give us pause (Bekoff, 2007; de Waal, 2019). From here, historicism derives some of its political importance. If myriad historical examples show us the contingency of human experience, constructed through situated and mutable conceptualisations of non-human others – animals, nature – then we ought to be able to use this critical impetus to disrupt the assumptions that undergird scientific work that would biologise and essentialise animal emotions and in turn expose the politics of this science. This should not be read as an intent necessarily to malign the politics of science, but simply to find another way to make those politics visible, to reveal the implicit affectivity of the ostensibly neutral. The practice of history has, to some extent, always been about keeping others – scientists, politicians,

---

[43] See also, Boddice, 2011a, especially the editor's introduction, 2011b.

[44] Barrett, (2017, 272–6), calls it the 'mental inference fallacy'. It is a circus mirror for behaviourism, reflecting one fallacy with its opposite, made more attractive because it appeals to human compassion and generosity in its politics. It has more generally been called anthropomorphism.

[45] See, for example, Darwin, 1872 and, even more concretely, Romanes, 1883. The genealogical lines can be traced, respectively, to Paul Ekman (1982) and his basic emotions acolytes and to philosopher and biomedical scientist Bernard Rollin (1989).

generals, journalists – honest. The new history of experience enhances the historian's capacity to do just this.

Third, history must take an active political role in the production of scientific knowledge concerning biological plasticity, extending from social neuroscience to microevolutionary and epigenetic research. The risk of not doing so is twofold: the rise of quackery and pseudoscience on the one hand, and a preponderance of culturally unreflexive 'hard' science on the other, coupled with unchallenged political appropriation. As Maurizio Meloni (2016) has observed, 'epigenetics has done away with the abstract universal body', with the risk of returning to nineteenth-century notions that 'specific biology' characterises 'local groups', which is fraught with racial, gender and class dangers. 'Especially in an age of increasing inequality', Meloni notes, 'political uses of epigenetics may ask if the poor suffer an ongoing accumulation of bad biology and whether this – as opposed to, for example, economic structures – is responsible for them slipping farther behind' (222). If historians are to embrace the historicity of experience in their own work, it seems essential also to prevent the essentialisation of experience in science, which is to say, in contemporary politics.[46]

5.3 Collaboration

If neuroscience has opened the door to the humanities, and to history especially, then emotion research cannot, as Daniel Gross and Stephanie Preston (2020) have shown in an article in *Emotion Review*, expect to carry on regardless. Gross is the author of *The Secret History of Emotion*; Preston is a cognitive neuroscientist. Their combination, therefore, has produced an entirely original historical argument that is aimed at revolutionising the way in which emotion science is done. Noting the influence of Charles Darwin's work on emotions, they demonstrate how far Darwin's method has been lost in the process of pinning specific psychological research goals on an eminent genealogy. Re-visiting Darwin's own method, they find fault with the current preoccupations with controls, delimitation of focus, and an overall level of specialism that leads to laboratory and experimental results that have no connection to the lived experience of emotions. Gross and Preston call for nothing less than a re-embrace of generalism within emotion science that would include the humanities in all

---

[46] See Lock and Palsson, 2016, who argue that epigenetics 'are bringing about an ontological shift ... in which nature and nurture are understood ... as always already mingled from the moment of conception' (12–13), and that science therefore cannot be left to have the field to itself, given that its findings implicate it in the humanities and social sciences. For an even more explicit statement to this end, and of the need to understand the body – biology – in situated, local and temporal context, see Lock, 2017.

aspects of emotion research, an insight they reach only through close historical analysis. Their exhortation to 'always historicise', seems like a fitting slogan for cross-disciplinary research. They have come up with a general rubric for emotion research that could begin to materially alter what we do, and what we do *together*.

Time will tell, of course, but for now, precisely how we might collaborate remains an open question. In the same issue as Gross and Preston's article, Otniel Dror (2020, 191) summarises his view of the historian's role across disciplinary lines, and highlights a specific challenge:

> The historian's contribution is . . . to make immanent in scientific emotion that which is missing from contemporary science: the cosmology, the vocation, the perspective of the humanities writ large. It is to exemplify how cultural assumptions are implicitly integrated into laboratory experiments. It is to explicate how (seemingly) natural kinds are, in fact, social kinds. It is to reconceive private acts (e.g., of 'irrationality') in terms of their social rationality. It is to demonstrate how our basic and intimate experiences are constituted in part by our moral-social valuations. It is to make ostensive the cultural scripting of seemingly reflex and pre-programmed physiological reactions. It is to challenge basic scientific tenets by studying the emotion-history of the science of emotions (rather than only the science-history of emotions). It is, in short, to infuse the historian's know-how into emotion . . . [The] foundational challenge for a science-humanities/bio-cultural emotion is . . . how do we infuse the know-how of the humanities into the laboratory and into scientific protocol?

How indeed? At this stage, we must continue to mutually engage with each other's work and to make collaborative pedagogical inroads where they are possible. This is by no means straightforward, but there must be a conviction that historians can make contributions to emotional, sensory and experiential knowledge per se, and not only as it concerns historiography. The first step, as we suggest in this Element, is to pursue the collapse of the distinction and the space between emotions history and sensory history. Not only does this afford us new historiographical possibilities in the history of experience, it better equips us to mobilise the knowledge we produce beyond our own disciplinary boundary. Indeed, the collapse of this space already *requires* a more interdisciplinary footing, but this must have implications for those other disciplines as well, to make theories, methods, practices and knowledge in a common space, including through teaching. If historians of emotion, sense and experience wait for a psychology with which they can agree 100 per cent, they will be waiting indefinitely. Our final question is what happens to the emotion knowledge produced by social neuroscience when it is collaboratively intersected with *ours*? We are not proposing to adopt, *in toto*, the theoretical framework of construction in neuroscience, but in fact to modify it by seeing what of it survives when mashed up with emotional, sensory and experiential historicism. We are not simply employing social neuroscientific theories for historiographical ends, but asking how both historiography and social neuroscience might change (and be taught) in the light of each other.

References

Ahn, Woo-Young, et al, 2014. 'Nonpolitical Images Evoke Neural Predictors of Political Ideology', *Current Biology*, 24, 27: 2693–9

Alford, J. R., C. L. Funk and J. R. Hibbing, 2005. 'Are Political Orientations Genetically Transmitted?' *American Political Science Review*, 99: 153–67

Ankersmit, Frank, 2018. 'Huizinga on Historical Experience', in *Senses and Sensations: Critical and Primary Sources*, David Howes, ed., vol. 2, 23–46, (London and New York: Bloomsbury Academic)

Aristotle, 1944. *Politics*, trans. H. Rackham (Cambridge, MA: Harvard University Press)

Bailey, Merridee L., and Katie Barclay, eds., 2017. *Emotion, Ritual and Power in Europe, 1200–1920: Family, State and Church* (London: Palgrave Macmillan)

Barrett, Lisa Feldman, 2006a. 'Are Emotions Natural Kinds?' *Perspectives on Psychological Science*, 1: 28–58

Barrett, Lisa Feldman, 2006b. 'Solving the Emotion Paradox: Categorization and the Experience of Emotion', *Personality and Social Psychology Review*, 10: 20–46

Barrett, Lisa Feldman, 2017. *How Emotions Are Made* (Boston and New York: Houghton Mifflin Harcourt).

Barrett, Lisa Feldman, Ralph Adolphs, Stacy Marsella, Aleix M. Martinex and Seth D. Pollak, 2019. 'Emotional Expressions Reconsidered: Challenges to Inferring Emotion From Human Facial Movements', *Psychological Science in the Public Interest*, 20: 1–68

Bekoff, Mark, 2007. *The Emotional Lives of Animals: A Leading Scientist Explores Animal Joy, Sorrow, and Empathy – and Why They Matter* (Novato, CA: New World Library)

Bessel, Richard, 2005. 'Hatred after War: Emotion and the Postwar History of East Germany',*History & Memory*, 17: 195–216

Bijsterveld, Karin, 2015. 'Ears-on Exhibitions: Sound in the History Museum', *The Public Historian*, 37, 73–90

Bloom, Paul, 2017. *Against Empathy: The Case for Rational Compassion* (New York: Random House)

Boddice, Rob, 2009. *A History of Attitudes and Behaviours toward Animals in Eighteenth- and Nineteenth-Century Britain: Anthropocentrism and the Emergence of Animals* (Lewiston, NY: Mellen Press)

Boddice, Rob, ed., 2011a. *Anthropocentrism: Humans, Animals, Environments* (Leiden: Brill)

Boddice, Rob, 2011b. 'The End of Anthropocentrism', in *Anthropocentrism: Humans, Animals, Environments*, ed. Rob Boddice (Leiden: Brill), 1–18

Boddice, Rob, 2013. 'Four Stages of Cruelty? Institutionalizing Humanity to Animals in the English Media, c.1750-1840', in *Mediale Konstruktionen*, ed. W. Behringer (*Studien zur Mediengeschichte*, vol. 1, Korb: Didymos-Verlag) 181–96

Boddice, Rob, ed., 2014. *Pain and Emotion in Modern History* (Houndmills: Palgrave)

Boddice, Rob, 2016. *The Science of Sympathy: Morality, Evolution and Victorian Civilization* (Urbana: University of Illinois Press)

Boddice, Rob, 2018a. *The History of Emotions* (Manchester: Manchester University Press)

Boddice, Rob, 2018b. 'Neurohistory', with commentary by Daniel Lord Smail, in *Debating New Approaches to History*, eds. Marek Tamm and Peter Burke (London: Bloomsbury) 301–25

Boddice, Rob, 2019a. 'Dispatches from the Emotional Rollercoaster', *Athenaeum Review*, 2: 98–101

Boddice, Rob, 2019b. 'The Developing Brain as Historical Artifact', *Developmental Psychology*, 55: 1994–7

Boddice, Rob, 2019c. *A History of Feelings* (London: Reaktion).

Boddice, Rob, 2019d. 'Hysteria or Tetanus? Ambivalent Embodiments and the Authenticity of Pain', in *Emotional Bodies: Studies on the Historical Performativity of Emotions*, eds. Dolores Martin Moruno and Beatriz Pichel (Urbana-Champaign: University of Illinois Press), 19–35

Boddice, Rob, 2021. *Humane Professions: The Defence of Experimental Medicine, 1876–1914* (Cambridge: Cambridge University Press)

Boddice, Rob, 2022. *Scientific and Medical Knowledge Production, 1796–1918: Experiment, Expertise, Experience*, 4 volumes (New York: Routledge)

Boquet, Damien, and Piroska Nagy, 2018. *Medieval Sensibilities: A History of Emotions in the Middle Ages* (Cambridge: Polity)

Bourke, Joanna, 2011. *What It Means to Be Human: Reflections from 1791 to the Present* (London: Virago)

Bourke, Joanna, 2014. *The Story of Pain: From Prayer to Painkillers* (Oxford: Oxford University Press)

Brauer, Juliane, and Martin Lücke, eds., 2013. *Emotionen, Geschichte und Historisches Lernen: Geschichtsdidaktische und Geschichtskulturelle Perspektiven* (Göttingen: V&R unipress)

Broomhall, Susan, ed., 2015. *Spaces for Feeling: Emotions and Sociabilities in Britain, 1650–1850* (New York: Routledge)

Brotherton, P. Sean, and Vinh-Kim Nguyen, 2013a. 'Revisiting Local Biology in the Era of Global Health', in 'Beyond the Body Proper: Global Politics/ Local Biology', special issue of *Medical Anthropology*, 32: 287–90

Brotherton, P. Sean, and Vinh-Kim Nguyen, eds, 2013b. 'Beyond the Body Proper: Global Politics/Local Biology', special issue of *Medical Anthropology*, 32

Brotons, Fanny H., 2017. 'The Experience of Cancer Illness: Spain and Beyond During the Second Half of the Nineteenth Century'. PhD Thesis, Carlos III University, Madrid

Burman, Jeremy T., 2012. 'History from Within? Contextualizing the New Neurohistory and Seeking Its Methods', *History of Psychology*, 15: 84–99

Burman, Jeremy T., 2014. 'Bringing the Brain into History: Behind Hunt's and Smail's Appeals to Neurohistory', in Cristian Tileagă and Jovan Byford, eds., *Psychology and History: Interdisciplinary Explorations*, 64–82 (Cambridge: Cambridge University Press)

Burstein, Andrew, 2001. 'The Political Character of Sympathy', *Journal of the Early Republic*, 21: 601–32

Cabanas, Edgar, and Eva Illouz, 2019. *Manufacturing Happy Citizens: How the Science and Industry of Happiness Control our Lives* (Cambridge: Wiley)

Carr, David, 2014. *Experience and History: Phenomenological Perspectives on the Historical World* (Oxford: Oxford University Press)

Carrera, Elena, 2014. 'Embodied Cognition and Empathy in Miguel de Cervantes's *El celoso extremeño*', *Hispania*, 97: 113–24.

Choudhury, S., and L. J. Kirmayer, 2009. 'Cultural Neuroscience and Psychopathology: Prospects for Cultural Psychiatry', *Progress in Brain Research*, 178: 263–83

Cicero, 1971. *On the Good Life*, trans. Michael Grant (New York: Penguin Books)

Cicero, 2000. *On Obligations*, trans. P. G. Walsh (New York: Oxford University Press)

Clark, Elizabeth B., 1995. '"The Sacred Rights of the Weak": Pain, Sympathy, and the Culture of Individual Rights in Antebellum America', *Journal of American History*, 82: 463–93

Clarke, Simon, Paul Hoggett and Simon Thompson, eds., 2006. *Emotion, Politics, and Society* (Houndmills: Palgrave)

Classen, Constance, 1993a. *Inca Cosmology and the Human Body* (Salt Lake City: University of Utah Press)

Classen, Constance, 1993b. *Worlds of Sense: Exploring the Senses in History and Across Cultures* (New York: Routledge)

Classen, Constance, 1997. 'Foundations for an Anthropology of the Senses', *International Social Science Journal*, 153: 401–12.

Classen, Constance, 1998. *The Color of Angels: Cosmology, Gender and the Aesthetic Imagination* (New York: Routledge)

Classen, Constance, ed., 2014. *A Cultural History of the Senses*, volumes 1–6 (New York: Bloomsbury)

Classen, Constance, and David Howes, 2006. 'The Museum as Sensescape: Western Sensibilities and Indigenous Artefacts', in Elizabeth Edwards, Chris Gosden and Ruth Phillips, eds., 199–222, *Sensible Objects: Colonialism, Museums and Material Culture* (New York: Berg)

Classen, Constance, David Howes and Anthony Synnott, 1994. *Aroma: The Cultural History of Smell* (New York: Routledge)

Collingwood, R.G., 1946. *The Idea of History* (Oxford: Oxford University Press, 1994)

Cooter, Roger, in press. 'The Importance of Gramsci Today: The 'New Lorians' and the Biological Reduction of History', in Massimiliano Badino and Pietro Daniel Omodeo, eds., *Cultural Hegemony in A Scientific World: Gramscian Concepts for the History of Science* (Leiden: Brill)

Corbin, Alain, 1986. *The Foul and the Fragrant: Odor and the French Social Imagination* (Cambridge: Harvard University Press)

Corbin, Alain, 1995. *Time, Desire and Horror: Towards a History of the Senses* (Cambridge: Polity Press)

Corbin, Alain, 2000. *Historien du sensible: Entretiens avec Gilles Heuré* (Paris: Découverte)

Cubitt, Geoffrey, 2014. 'History, Psychology and Social Memory',in Cristian Tileagă and Jovan Byford, eds., *Psychology and History: Interdisciplinary Explorations*, 15–39 (Cambridge: Cambridge University Press)

Darwin, Charles, 1872. *The Expression of Emotions in Man and Animals* (London: John Murray)

Davis, Jr., O. L., 2001. 'In Pursuit of Historical Empathy', in Ozro Luke Davis, Elizabeth Anne Yeager and Stuart J. Foster, eds., *Historical Empathy and Perspective Taking in the Social Studies*, (Lanham, MD: Rowman & Littlefield) 1–12

Delville, Michel, Andrew Norris and Viktoria Von Hoffmann, eds., 2015. *Le Dégoût. Histoire, langage, esthétique et politique d'une émotion plurielle* (Liège: Presses Universitaires de Liège)

Dilthey, William, 2002. *The Formation of the Historical World in the Human Sciences* (Princeton: Princeton University Press)

Dixon, Thomas, 2011. 'Sensibility and History. The Importance of Lucien Febvre'. The History of Emotions Blog, https://emotionsblog .history.qmul.ac.uk/2011/11/sensibility-and-history-the-importance-of-lucien-febvre/

Downes, Stephanie, Sally Holloway and Sarah Randles, eds., 2018. *Feeling Things: Objects and Emotions through History* (Oxford: Oxford University Press)

Dray, William H., 1995. *History as Re-enactment: R.G. Collingwood's Idea of History* (Oxford: Oxford University Press)

Dror, Otniel, 2020. 'Historians in the Emotion Laboratory', *Emotion Review*, 12: 191–2.

Ekman, Paul, 1982. *Emotion in the Human Face* (Cambridge: Cambridge University Press)

Eustace, Nicole, 2008. *Passion is the Gale: Emotion, Power, and the Coming of the American Revolution* (Chapel Hill: University of North Carolina Press)

Evans, Richard J., 1997. *In Defence of History* (London: Granta)

Febvre, Lucien, 1938. 'Une vue d'ensemble: Histoire et psychologie', in *Combats pour l'Histoire*, Paris: Armand Colin.

Febvre, Lucien, 1941. 'La sensibilité et l'histoire: Comment reconstituer la vie affective d'autrefois ?' *Annales d'Histoire Sociale*, 3 (1–2): 5–20

Febvre, Lucien, 1947. *Le problème de l'incroyance au XVIe siècle. La religion de Rabelais* (Paris: Albin Michel)

Febvre, Lucien, 1973. 'Sensibility and History: How to Reconstitute the Emotional Life of the Past', in Peter Burke, ed., trans K. Folca, *A New Kind of History and Other Essays*, 12–26 (New York: Harper)

Febvre, Lucien, 1982. *The Problem of Unbelief in the Sixteenth Century: The Religion of Rabelais*, trans. Beatrice Gottlieb (Cambridge, MA: Harvard University Press)

Frevert, Ute, 2011. *Emotions: Lost and Found* (Budapest: Central European University Press)

Fuchs, Thomas, 2018. *Ecology of the Brain: The Phenomenology and Biology of the Embodied Brain* (Oxford: Oxford University Press)

Geier, Ted, 2017. *Meat Markets: The Cultural History of Bloody London* (Edinburgh: Edinburgh University Press)

Gendron, M., K. A. Lindquist, L. Barsalou and L. F. Barrett, 2012. 'Emotion Words Shape Emotion Percepts', *Emotion*, 12: 314–25.

Godfrey, Sima, 2002. 'Alain Corbin: Making Sense of French History', *French Historical Studies*, 25: 381–98

Griffin, Emma, 2005. *England's Revelry: A History of Popular Sports and Pastimes, 1660–1830* (Oxford: Oxford University Press)

Gross, Daniel M., and Stephanie D. Preston, 2020. 'Darwin and the Situation of Emotion Research', *Emotion Review*, 12: 179–90

Halttunen, Karen, 1995. 'Humanitarianism and the Pornography of Pain in Anglo-American Culture', *American Historical Review*, 100: 303–34

Hartman, Saidiya, 1997. *Scenes of Subjection: Terror, Slavery, and Self-Making in Nineteenth Century America* (Oxford: Oxford University Press)

Hartman, Saidiya, 2007. *Lose Your Mother: A Journey along the Atlantic Slave Route* (New York: Farrar, Straus and Giroux)

Haskell, Thomas L., 1985. 'Capitalism and the Origins of the Humanitarian Sensibility', parts I and II, *American Historical Review*, 90: 339–61, 547–66

Henshaw, Victoria, 2013. *Urban Smellscapes: Understanding and Designing City Smell Environments* (New York: Routledge)

Hinton, James, 2011. *Nine Wartime Lives: Mass Observation and the Making of the Modern Self* (Oxford: Oxford University Press.

Hitzer, Bettina, 2020a. 'The Odor of Disgust: Contemplating the Dark Side of 20th-Century Cancer History', *Emotion Review*, 12: 156–67

Hitzer, Bettina, 2020b. *Krebs fühlen: Eine Emotionsgeschichte des 20. Jahrhunderts* (Stuttgart: Klett-Cotta)

Hoemann, Katie, Madeleine Devlin and Lisa Feldman Barrett, 2020. 'Comment: Emotions Are Abstract, Conceptual Categories That Are Learned by a Predicting Brain', *Emotion Review*

Hoemann, Katie, F. Xu and L.F. Barrett, 2019. 'Emotion Words, Emotion Concepts, and Emotional Development in Children: A Constructionist Hypothesis', *Developmental Psychology*, 55: 1830–49

Howes, David, 1989. 'Scent and Sensibility', *Culture, Medicine and Psychiatry*, 13: 81–9

Howes, David, 1990. 'Controlling Textuality: A Call for a Return to the Senses', *Anthropologica*, 33: 55–73

Howes, David, ed., 1991. *The Varieties of Sensory Experience: A Sourcebook in the Anthropology of the Senses* (Toronto: University of Toronto Press)

Howes, David, 2018a. 'Introduction: On the History and Sociology of the Senses', in David Howes, ed., *Senses and Sensations: Critical and Primary Sources*, vol. 2 (London and New York: Bloomsbury Academic), 1–20

Howes, David, 2018b. 'Introduction: On the Individuation/Integration of the Senses in the Fields of Biology, Psychology and Neuroscience – An Orthogonal View', in David Howes, ed., *Senses and Sensation: Critical and Primary Sources. Biology, Psychology and Neuroscience*, vol. 3, 1–32 (New York: Bloomsbury)

Huizinga, Johan. 1919. *Herfsttij der Middeleeuwen: Studie Over Levens-en Gedachtenvormen der Veertiende en Vijftiende Eeuw in Frankkrijk en de Nederlanden*, www.gutenberg.org/cache/epub/16829/pg16829.txt

Huizinga, Johan, 1984. 'The Task of Cultural History', in his *Men and Ideas: History, the Middle Ages, the Renaissance* (Princeton, NJ: Princeton University Press), 17–76.

Huizinga, Johan, 2009. *The Waning of the Middle Ages* (n.p.: Benediction Classics)

Hunt, Lynn, 2009. 'The Experience of Revolution', *French Historical Studies*, 32: 671–8

Hunt, Nigel C., 2012. *Memory, War and Trauma* (Cambridge: Cambridge University Press)

Illouz, Eva, 2007. *Cold Intimacies: The Making of Emotional Capitalism* (Cambridge: Wiley)

Inbar, Yoel, David Pizzaro, Ravi Iyer and Jonathan Haidt, 2012. 'Disgust Sensitivity, Political Conservatism, and Voting', *Social Psychological and Personality Science*, 3: 537–44

Jay, Martin, 2006. *Songs of Experience: Modern American and European Variations on a Universal Theme* (Berkeley: University of California Press)

Johnson, Samuel, 1768. *A Dictionary of the English Language*, 3rd ed. (Dublin: Thomas Ewing)

Jost, J. T., C. M. Federico, and J. L. Napier, 2009. 'Political Ideology: Its Structure, Functions, and Elective Affinities', *Annual Review of Psychology*, 60: 307–37

Jütte, Robert, 2005. *A History of the Senses: From Antiquity to Cyberspace* (Cambridge: Polity Press)

Jütte, Robert, 2019. 'Reodorizing the Modern Age', in Mark M. Smith, ed., *Smell and History: A Reader* (Morgantown: West Virginia University Press)

Kaster, Robert A., 2005. *Emotion, Restraint, and Community in Ancient Rome* (Oxford: Oxford University Press), 170–86

Kerr, Heather, David Lemmings and Robert Phiddian, eds., 2016. *Passions, Sympathy and Print Culture: Public Opinion and Emotional Authenticity in Eighteenth-Century Britain* (London: Palgrave Macmillan)

Kiechle, Melanie, 2017. *Smell Detectives: An Olfactory History of Nineteenth-Century Urban America* (Seattle: University of Washington Press)

Kirmayer, L. J., and D. Crafa, 2014. 'What Kind of Science for Psychiatry?', *Frontiers in Human Neuroscience*, 8: 435.

Kirmayer, Laurence J., Carol M. Worthman, Shinobu Kitayama, Robert Lemelson and Constance Cummings, eds., 2020. *Culture, Mind, and Brain: Emerging Concepts, Models, Applications* (Cambridge: Cambridge University Press)

Kitchener, Andrew C., 2018. 'Making Sense of the Senses across Species Boundaries: Curating the Animal Senses Gallery at National Museums Scotland', in *Senses and Sensation*, ed. Howes, vol. 3, 363–74

Kolnai, Aurel, 2004. *On Disgust*, eds. Barry Smith and Carolyn Korsmeyer (Chicago: Open Court)

Koselleck, Reinhart, 2002. *The Practice of Conceptual History: Timing History, Spacing Concepts*, trans. Todd Samuel Presner (Stanford: Stanford University Press)

Kounine, Laura, 2018. *Imagining the Witch: Emotions, Gender, and Selfhood in Early Modern Germany* (Oxford: Oxford University Press)

Kuntsman, Adi, 2009. '"With a Shade of Disgust": Affective Politics of Sexuality and Class in Memoirs of the Stalinist Gulag', *Slavic Review*, 68: 308–28

LaCapra, Dominic, 2009. *History and Its Limits: Human, Animal, Violence* (Ithaca: Cornell University Press)

Lanzoni, Susan, 2018. *Empathy: A History* (New Haven: Yale University Press)

Lateiner, D., and D. Spatharas, eds., 2016. *The Ancient Emotion of Disgust* (Oxford: Oxford University Press)

Lawrence-Lightfoot, Sara, and Jessica Hoffman Davis, 1997. *The Art and Science of Portraiture* (San Francisco: Jossey-Bass)

Leys, Ruth, 2017. *The Ascent of Affect: Genealogy and Critique* (Chicago: University of Chicago Press)

Lock, Margaret, and Gisli Palsson, 2016. *Can Science Resolve the Nature/ Nurture Debate?* (Oxford: Polity)

Lock, Margaret, 1993. *Encounters with Aging: Mythologies of Menopause in Japan and North America* (Berkeley: University of California Press)

Lock, Margaret, 2017. 'Recovering the Body', *Annual Review of Anthropology*, 46: 1–14

Lydon, Jane, 2020. *Imperial Emotions: The Politics of Empathy across the British Empire* (Cambridge: Cambridge University Press)

Massumi, Brian, 2018. 'What Animals Teach Us about Politics', in *Senses and Sensation*, ed. Howes, vol. 3, 279–89

Matich, Olga, 2009. 'Poetics of Disgust: To Eat and Die in Andrei Belyi's Petersburg', *Slavic Review*, 68: 284–307.

Matt, Susan J., and Peter N. Stearns, eds., 2013. *Doing Emotions History* (Urbana: University of Illinois Press)

McAuliffe, Kathleen, 2019. 'The Yuck Factor', *The Atlantic*, www.theatlantic.com/magazine/archive/2019/03/the-yuck-factor/580465/

McGrath, L. S., 2017. 'Historiography, Affect, and the Neurosciences', *History of Psychology*, 20: 129–47

Meloni, Maurizio, 2016. *Political Biology: Science and Social Values in Human Heredity from Eugenics to Epigenetics* (Houndmills: Palgrave)

Meloni, Maurizio, 2019. *Impressionable Biologies: From the Archaeology of Plasticity to the Sociology of Epigenetics* (New York: Routledge)

Millard, Chris, 2020. 'Using Personal Experience in the Academic Medical Humanities: A Genealogy', *Social Theory & Health*, 18: 184–98

Moscoso, Javier, 2012. *Pain: A Cultural History* (Houndmills: Palgrave)

Moscoso, Javier, and Juan Manuel Zaragoza, 2014. 'Historias del bienstar. Desde la historia de las emociones a las políticas de la experiencia', *Cuadernos de Historia Contemporánea*, 36: 73–88

Moscoso, Javier, 2016. 'From the History of Emotions to the History of Experience: A Republican Sailor's Sketchbook in the Civil War', in Luisa Elena Delgado, Pura Fernandez and Jo Labanyi, eds., *Engaging the Emotions in Spanish Culture and History* (Nashville: Vanderbilt University Press), 176–91

Neuman, W. Russell, et al., eds, 2007. *The Affect Effect: Dynamics of Emotion in Political Thinking and Behavior* (Chicago)

Newton, Hannah, 2018. *Misery to Mirth: Recovery from Illness in Early Modern England* (Oxford: Oxford University Press)

Olsen, Stephanie, and Rob Boddice, 2017. 'Styling Emotions History', *Journal of Social History*, 51: 476–87

Otterspeer, Willem, 2010. *Reading Huizinga* (Amsterdam: Amsterdam University Press)

Parr, Joy, 2010. *Sensing Changes: Technologies, Environments, and the Everyday, 1953–2003* (Vancouver: University of British Columbia Press)

Parrott, Gerrod W., 2016. 'Psychological Perspectives on Emotion in Groups', in *Passions, Sympathy and Print Culture: Public Opinion and Emotional Authenticity in Eighteenth-century Britain*, eds. Kerr, Lemmings, and Phiddian, 20–44

Pernau, Margrit, and Imke Rajamani, 2016. 'Emotional Translations: Conceptual History Beyond Language', *History and Theory*, 55: 46–65

Plamper, Jan, 2015. *The History of Emotions: An Introduction* (Oxford: Oxford University Press)

Plato, (2000), *The Republic*, trans. Tom Griffith (Cambridge: Cambridge University Press)

Rabin, Roni Caryn, 2020. 'Lost Sense of Smell Could Be A Peculiar Clue to Coronavirus Infection', *Economic Times*, March 23. https://economictimes .indiatimes.com/news/international/world-news/lost-sense-of-smell-may-be -peculiar-clue-to-coronavirus-infection/articleshow/74767666.cms

Rajamani, Imke, 2016. 'Angry Young Men: Masculinity, Citizenship and Virtuous Emotions in Popular Indian Cinema', PhD Thesis, Freie Universität Berlin

Reddy, William M., 2000. 'Sentimentalism and Its Erasure: The Role of Emotions in the Era of the French Revolution', *Journal of Modern History*, 72: 109–52

Reddy, William M., 2001. *The Navigation of Feeling: A Framework for the History of Emotions* (Cambridge: Cambridge University Press)

Reddy, William M., 2020. 'The Unavoidable Intentionality of Affect: The History of Emotions and the Neurosciences of the Present-Day', *Emotion Review.*

Retz, Tyson, 2018. *Empathy and History: Historical Understanding in Re-enactment, Hermeneutics and Education* (New York: Berghahn Books)

Rollin, Bernard, 1989. *The Unheeded Cry: Animal Consciousness, Animal Pain and Scientific Change* (Oxford: Oxford University Press)

Romanes, George John, 1883. *Animal Intelligence*, 3rd ed. (London: Kegan Paul, Trench)

Rosenfeld, Sophia, 2011. 'On Being Heard: A Case for Paying Attention to the Historical Ear', *American Historical Review*, 116 (2): 316–34

Rosenwein, Barbara, 2016. *Generations of Feeling: A History of Emotions, 600–1700* (Cambridge: Cambridge University Press)

Rosenwein, Barbara, and Riccardo Cristiani, 2018. *What Is the History of Emotions?* (Cambridge: Polity)

Scheer, Monique, 2012. 'Are Emotions a Kind of Practice (and Is That What Makes Them Have a History)? A Bourdieuian Approach to Understanding Emotion', *History and Theory*, 51: 193–220

Scott, Joan W., 1991. 'The Evidence of Experience', *Critical Inquiry*, 17: 773–97

Shortall, Sarah, 2014. 'Psychedelic Drugs and the Problem of Experience', *Past & Present*, 222 (suppl9): 187–206.

Smail, Daniel Lord, 2008. *On Deep History and the Brain* (Berkeley: University of California Press)

Smith, Mark M., 2001. *Listening to Nineteenth-Century America* (Chapel Hill: University of North Carolina Press)

Smith, Mark M., 2007a. 'Producing Sense, Consuming Sense, Making Sense: Perils and Prospects for Sensory History', *Journal of Social History*, 40: 841–58

Smith, Mark M., 2007b. *Sensing the Past: Seeing, Hearing, Smelling, Tasting, and Touching in History* (Berkeley: University of California Press)

Smith, Mark M., 2010. 'Looking Back: The Explosion of Sensory History', *The Psychologist*, 28, 860–63

Smith, Mark M., 2012. 'Transcending, Othering, Detecting: Smell, Premodernity, Modernity', *Postmedieval: A Journal of Medieval Cultural Studies*, 3 (4): 380–90

Smith, Mark M., 2015a. *The Smell of Battle, The Taste of War: A Sensory History of the Civil War* (New York: Oxford University Press)

Smith, Mark M., 2015b. 'Sound – So What?' *The Public Historian*, 37, 132–44

Smith, Mark M., forthcoming. *A Sensory History Manifesto*

Stearns, Carol Z., and Peter N. Stearns, 1986. *Anger: The Struggle for Emotional Control in America's History* (Chicago: University of Chicago Press)

Stearns, Carol Z. and Peter N. Stearns, eds., 1988. *Emotion and Social Change: Toward a New Psychohistory* (New York: Holmes & Meier)

Steintrager, James A., 2004. *Cruel Delight: Enlightenment Culture and the Inhuman* (Bloomington: Indiana University Press)

Stenner, Paul, 2017.*Liminality and Experience: A Transdisciplinary Approach to the Psychosocial* (Houndmills: Palgrave)

Sullivan, Erin, 2016. *Beyond Melancholy: Sadness and Selfhood in Renaissance England* (Oxford: Oxford University Press)

Torre, Jose R., 2007. *The Political Economy of Sentiment: Paper Credit and the Scottish Enlightenment in Early Republic Boston, 1780–1820* (London)

Tsakiris, Manos, and Helena de Presster, eds., 2018. *The Interoceptive Mind: From Homeostasis to Awareness* (Oxford: Oxford University Press)

Umbach, Maiken, and Mathew Humphrey, 2018. *Authenticity: The Cultural History of a Political Concept* (Cham: Palgrave Macmillan)

Vallgårda, Karen, Kristine Alexander and Stephanie Olsen, 2015. 'Emotions and the Global Politics of Childhood', in *Childhood, Youth and Emotions in Modern History*, ed. Stephanie Olsen (Houndmills: Palgrave), 12–34

Vallgårda, Karen, Kristine Alexander and Stephanie Olsen, 2018. 'Against Agency', www.shcy.org/features/commentaries/against-agency/

Waal, Frans de, 2019. *Mama's Last Hug: Animal Emotions and What They Tell Us about Ourselves* (New York: W.W. Norton)

Webster, Noah, 1832. *A Dictionary of the English Language* (London: Black, Young and Young)

White, Hayden, 1973. *Metahistory: The Historical Imagination in Nineteenth-Century Europe* (Baltimore: Johns Hopkins University Press)

White, Hayden, 1974. 'The Historical Text as Literary Artifact', *Clio*, 3: 277–91.

Whitehouse and Pieter François, 2017. 'Afterword: Ritual, Emotion and Power', in *Emotion, Ritual and Power in Europe*, eds. Bailey and Barclay.

Winter, Jay, 2016. 'From Sympathy to Empathy: Trajectories of Rights in the Twentieth Century', in Aleida Assmann and Ines Detmers, eds., *Empathy and its Limits*, (Houndmills: Palgrave), 100–114

Woods, Michael, 2011. '"The Indignation of Freedom-Loving People": The Caning of Charles Sumner and Emotion in Antebellum Politics', *Journal of Social History*, 44: 609–705

Woods, Michael, 2014. *Emotional and Sectional Conflict in the Antebellum United States* (Cambridge: Cambridge University Press)

Young, Allan, 2012. 'Empathic Cruelty and the Origins of the Social Brain', in Suparna Choudhury and Jan Slaby, eds., *Critical Neuroscience: A Handbook of the Social and Cultural Contexts of Neuroscience*, (Oxford: Blackwell), 159–76

Zitner, Aaron, John McCormick and Dante Chinni, 2020. 'How Coronavirus Is Breaking Down Along Familiar Political Lines', *Wall Street Journal*, April 4, www.wsj.com/articles/how-coronavirus-is-breaking-down-along-familiar-political-lines-11586001600

Acknowledgements

The authors thank Jan Plamper and Liz Friend-Smith for soliciting this manuscript and encouraging its swift production. For Rob Boddice, core ideas were tested at the first annual conference of the Finnish Academy Centre of Excellence for the History of Experiences (HEX) in Tampere, Finland, in March 2019 and at the research seminar of the Centre for the History of Emotions at Queen Mary, University of London, in November 2019. My thanks to Ville Kivimäki, Rhodri Heyward, Peter Stearns and Susan Matt in particular, and to Pertti Haapala, Thomas Dixon and Tiffany Watt Smith for facilitating some challenging discussions. The Element has been written under the auspices of the European Union's Horizon 2020 research and innovation programme under the Marie Sklodowska-Curie grant agreement No. 742470. Eternal gratitude to Stephanie Olsen and to Sébastien, as ever. For their inspiration and collegiality, I dedicate the work to my colleagues at HEX.

Mark Smith remains grateful for a Provost's Humanities Grant awarded by the University of South Carolina, which gave him valuable time to write. For offering him congenial spaces in which to test his ideas, he remains indebted to the Music and Culture Colloquium Series (University of South Carolina, February 2020); Dr Lesa Scholl of Kathleen Lumley College, Adelaide, Australia (May 2019); the History Department at the University of Adelaide, Australia (May 2019); and to Dr Tim Lockley of the School of Comparative American Studies at the University of Warwick, UK who invited him to think about the senses and emotions for a Distinguished Lecture Series Keynote Address in November 2018.

Cambridge Elements $\equiv$

Histories of Emotions and the Senses

Jan Plamper

Goldsmiths, University of London

Jan Plamper is Professor of History at Goldsmiths, University of London, where he teaches an MA seminar on the history of emotions. His publications include *The History of Emotions: An Introduction* (2015), a multidisciplinary volume on fear with contributors from neuroscience to horror film to the 1929 stock market crash, and articles on the sensory history of the Russian Revolution and the history of soldiers' fears in World War I. He has also authored *The Stalin Cult: A Study in the Alchemy of Power* (2012) and, in German, *The New We. Why Migration Is No Problem: A Different History of the Germans* (2019).

About the Series

Born of the emotional and sensory "turns," Elements in Histories of Emotions and the Senses move one of the fastest-growing interdisciplinary fields forward. The series is aimed at scholars across the humanities, social sciences, and life sciences, embracing insights from a diverse range of disciplines, from neuroscience to art history and economics. Chronologically and regionally broad, encompassing global, transnational, and deep history, it concerns such topics as affect theory, intersensoriality, embodiment, human-animal relations, and distributed cognition.

Cambridge Elements ≡

Histories of Emotions and the Senses

Printed in the United States
By Bookmasters